FROM THE SACRED HEART TO THE TRINITY

The Spiritual Itinerary of
Saint Teresa Margaret of the
Sacred Heart, O.C.D.

Father Gabriel of St. Mary Magdalene, O.C.D.

Translated by

Rev. Sebastian V. Ramge, O.C.D.

ICS Publications
Institute of Carmelite Studies
Washington, DC
2006

ICS Publications
2131 Lincoln Road, NE
Washington, DC 20002-1199
www.icspublications.org

Typeset and produced in the United States of America

Library of Congress Cataloging-in-Publication Data

Gabriele di Santa Maria Maddalena, Father.
    [Du Sacre-Coeur a la Trinite. English]
    From the Sacred Heart to the Trinity: the spiritual itinerary of Saint Teresa
    Margaret of the Sacred Heart, O.C.D./ by Father Gabriel of St. Mary
    Magdalene; Translated by Sebastian V. Ramge.
       p. cm.
    Originally published: Milwaukee, Wis.: Spiritual Life Press, c1965.
    Includes bibliographical references.
    ISBN 0-935216-37-5 (alk. paper)
    1. Teresa Margaret of the Sacred Heart, Saint, 1747-1770. I. Title.
    BX4700.T43G3313 2005
    282'.092--dc22
                         2005011079

CONTENTS

FROM THE SACRED HEART TO THE TRINITY

Foreword

The systematic analysis of the process of beatification of Anna Maria Redi, in religion Sister Teresa Margaret of the Sacred Heart of Jesus, presents a worthwhile reward to us: it reveals the soul of the Saint.

In spite of her recent canonization (1934), Saint Teresa Margaret is still almost completely unknown by our contemporaries. Many biographies are incomplete to the point of almost being insignificant. This is an odd fact, for we do not hesitate to rank her among the primary figures who represent the glory of Carmel—among Teresa of Jesus, John of the Cross, and Thérèse of the Child Jesus.

The great interval between the decree proclaiming the heroism of her virtues (1839) and the decree of her beatification (1929) explains why the wealth of material contained in the informative process was allowed to slip into the shadow when the Saint was presented to the general public on the occasion of her beatification. People no longer knew about these processes that served only to examine and demonstrate the heroism of her virtues; after 1839 they were no longer of any use. We have had the good fortune of discovering the "public copy"[1] in the archives of the Postulator of the Discalced Carmelite Order. Upon examination these processes revealed very valuable information, for they enable us to reconstruct the entire spiritual itinerary of the Saint with surprising certitude and clarity. We shall attempt in this study to give the main points: they will suffice to place before us a person of a truly singular grandeur.

The "public copy" of the process of Saint Teresa Margaret comprises nine large volumes written in a legible hand. The first five volumes contain the Informative Process; three others give an account of the Apostolic Process "concerning her virtues"; the last one gives us the Apostolic Process "concerning the fame of her sanctity." It is the Informative Process that is most rewarding. It was begun in 1773, three years after the death of the Saint; ten years were required to examine the witnesses. These witnesses are of primary importance, both in regard to the period of the Saint's life passed in the world as well as that which she lived in the monastery.

For the earlier period (1747–1764) we have her father who represents the family center, two religious governesses, and one of the confessors who directed her from the period of time the Saint spent as a boarding pupil at Saint Apollina's, and the lady with whom she stayed during the two months spent outside the monastery after her postulancy (January and February 1765).

We have several important witnesses to tell us about the years the Saint spent in the Carmel of Florence: her superior during almost the entire time the Saint spent there (Mother Anna Maria Piccolomini); two novitiate companions (Sister Teresa Maria Ricasoli and Sister Maria Victoria Martini); and Sister Magdalene Teresa Vecchietti, a companion. Two of the confessors who directed her gave their depositions: Father Valerian of Saint Lawrence and Father Ildephonse of Saint Louis, her spiritual father.

Father Ildephonse was a man of remarkable insight, and his testimony at the process is so abundant that it fills a volume and a half. He is, therefore, the chief witness. After him in importance comes Mother Anna Maria Piccolomini whose testimony fills an entire volume of the Informative Process.

The Apostolic Processes (1817–1830) are, in their turn, very important not only because they introduce us to contemporary witnesses: the brother and sister of the Saint, another novitiate companion (Sister Teresa of the Crucified Albergotti) and others who knew her personally at Saint Apollina's or during her trip to La Verna, but particularly because they contain an ample supply of documents officially gathered in three environments very important in the life of the Saint: the monastery of Saint Apollina's, the monastery of Saint Teresa's in which she lived, and the convent of the Carmelite Friars of Saint Paulinus in Florence where her superiors and spiritual directors lived. They permit us to supplement frequently the oral testimonies of the process with documentary proofs and thus to give them a new and stronger foundation. In this work of reconstructing the spiritual journey of the Saint we shall rely almost exclusively upon this double source of information.

The life of the Saint is distinguished exteriorly by two periods, the first of which includes the years preceding her entrance into Carmel (July 15, 1747 to August 31, 1764), and the second comprising the years she spent in the Teresian monastery (September 1, 1764 to March 7, 1770).

In the first period we can distinguish the years spent in her father's house at Arezzo (until November 1759—a period of nine years); the years spent in the boarding school attached to the Benedictine monastery of Saint Apollina in Florence (November 1759 until April 1764); the remaining months spent in her father's house at Arezzo (April 1764 to the end of August 1764).

The period of her monastic life began with a four-month postulancy (September 1, 1764 to January 4, 1765); the next two months were spent outside the cloister (January 4 to March 11, 1765) and finally, five years of religious life properly speaking (until her death on March 7, 1770). The only noteworthy date of her exterior life is her profession day (March 12, 1766), followed in a few days by her taking of the veil (April 9, 1766).

In this brief human career of twenty-two years and eight months there was a magnificent spiritual flight which carried our Saint to the highest peaks of the mystical life—a mystical life completely devoid of extraordinary graces but of singular depth. Anna Maria Redi, Sister Teresa Margaret of the Sacred Heart of Jesus, is of the purest lineage: the hidden flame of infused love that burned and consumed her illumined and directed her entire life, leading her to the heights of the Trinitarian life. Then it expanded into a most ardent contemplative apostolate. I am eager to add the fact that she never read the works of the Mystical Doctor (Saint John of the Cross) and yet—which is amazing—there is a most striking resemblance between them!

Her spiritual journey also has two distinct periods that are separated from one another by an eminent grace. This grace transformed to some degree her manner of journeying to God by introducing a marked passivity. It is a grace that, let us say, providentially permitted the profound effects it wrought in her soul to escape to the surface a little. This is really a remarkable thing in a soul so devoted to the hidden life as Saint Teresa Margaret was. There is a characteristic mark of the Saint that, although a small one, is seldom commented upon: the mystical grace received one Sunday morning while she was assisting at the recitation of Terce in choir. At the capitulum (little lesson) Teresa Margaret heard the words "Deus caritas est ..." ("God is love ...") and immediately she felt herself being overcome by a surge of divine love that was to absorb her in God for several days afterward. From that date there was something profoundly changed in her: she lived thereafter under a divine influence that was to continue augmenting in her to the day of her death. Consequently, we feel it correct to call this period of her life the mystical period, reserving the name of the ascetical period to the years preceding this grace wherein she directed herself to God by an effort that is obviously personal. We do not wish, however, to exclude from this earlier period, wherein the Saint already appears to be a contemplative, the influence of infused knowledge and love, just as in the mystical period we will find that the Saint worked ardently to realize her ideal of love. The qualifications we use are only intended to describe the overall cast of each period.

The witnesses do not agree on the date to be assigned to the grace signaling her entrance into the second period. From the ensemble of the testimonies of the witnesses and the various documents, it seems that we might hazard placing the date with certitude during the months of January or February 1767, a period three years prior to her death. We shall give our reasons for assigning this date later in our study. At that time the Saint was nineteen and a half years old.

The years preceding the grace of "Deus caritas est" correspond to the period that we are going to call the ascetical period. It comprises, in addition to the years spent in the family circle and at school at Saint Apollina's, two and a half years spent in Carmel. If we wish to indicate the date that, more or less, can be assigned to the beginning of the period, we must go back to the fifth year of the Saint's life. Father Ildephonse is our witness that from this early age Teresa Margaret dedicated herself completely to a life of love of God. And no one is more capable of such a statement than her spiritual director. He was not content with merely sitting back and watching her spiritual growth; he would often prudently question her and with great diligence would exact an account of her efforts and advancement. He has left us his judgment of the whole journey, and these documents permit us to follow her spiritual progress with most rigorous exactitude:

"From the first moments of the use of reason ... she was so dominated (by love of God) that she was unable to wish or love or do or seek anything which was not God or for God, and this divine fire increased in her to such a point that she was unable to encounter any obstacle which could prevent her progress. Her physical death itself was the final victory fully consummated by that hidden embrace; so much so, in fact, that we can apply to her (according to the interpretation of Saint Augustine) the words of Deuteronomy: 'Dominus Deus tuus ignis consumens est' ('The Lord thy God is a consuming fire'— Dt 4:24)."

One could not better describe the life of this Saint: she was literally consumed by divine love—by the active love that she nourished in her heart and by the passive love that pervaded and inundated her in the latter part of her life and that ravaged her in an "implacable" manner. No other word seems satisfactory in attempting to characterize the work of divine love in her.

It is our task then to narrate what is essentially a "life of love," of ascetic and mystic love, of contemplative and apostolic love, but one that still attains the heights in all these aspects.

In the ascetic period we are going to assist at the awakening of the Spouse in her heart in her home, at her maturing in the monastery of Saint Apollina, at her first blossoming during the months spent at Arezzo in the family circle, and her joyous expanding in the atmosphere of the Teresian cloister.

The mystic period will mark a lofty flight in the midst of sorrow that is nothing other than a suffering of love: we will contemplate her birth, admire the generous reaction of the Saint inspiring her to offer herself as a victim of love; we will assist at the implacable overwhelming of consuming love that will allow her to pass, without stopping, through the stopping places and that will lead her, although astonishingly young, to the most elevated peaks which melt into the eternal "determination."

In order to avoid prolonging this study too much, we are going to pass rather rapidly over the ascetic period, contenting ourselves by making note only of the most characteristic marks therein, so that we can devote ourselves to the period that was marked by an ever more overwhelming divine influence, in which Sister Teresa Margaret sanctified herself.

Note

[1] The "public copy" of the Process of Beatification was the official transcription of all the various testimonies of the process made in every diocese where the Servant of God lived. It was made under the meticulous direction of the Congregation of Rites. This legal transcription was given to the Postulator of the Cause who prepared a summary of the person's life used at the deliberations of the Congregation.

Part I
The Ascetical Period

Father Ildephonse assures us that, from the very moment in which she understood Who God is, the Saint immediately loved Him. He learned this from the lips of the Saint herself. "But just as everyone else does!" she replied artlessly to the priest who asked her if she had done this without any delay. She was convinced that this was a natural phenomenon for all Christian souls. "She turned immediately towards this great God," testifies Father Ildephonse, "not only by recognizing in Him the Lord of all, but also by loving Him above everything else since He is the sovereign good; seeing that He was her last end, she surrendered herself to Him by seeking His good pleasure and glory in her affections and in her works during the entire course of her life, regardless of what she did."

In addition Father quotes verbatim—he seems to have had an excellent memory—the words of the Saint: "Jesus well knows that, since my infancy, I have never desired anything except to please Him and advance in holiness."

She was about five years old when she made this admirable "choice" that was to determine her entire life—she would be "all for God." The consequences of this choice soon became manifest: she was completely occupied with Him.

Several testimonies corroborate to illustrate this point.

Anna Maria was six years old when, as testifies an aunt on her father's side—a woman of great piety, who was lodging for a time in their home—many a time she was seen to "keep her eyes fixed upward for long periods of time as if she were meditating upon the grandeurs of God and were offering Him her love with her whole heart."

The Saint's brother, Francis Xavier, who was four years younger than she, tells us a delightful story of a childhood incident from this same period. "One day I wanted to go to the playroom to join my little brothers who were playing there noisily. While crawling up the stairs, I recognized my sister Teresa, then called Anna, sitting to the right between two windows on the landing. She was knitting a stocking, her eyes lowered in prayer. She was so absorbed in God, as I now recall, that she made no sign of having noticed me. I stopped to watch her, forgetting about my brothers, and, seeing her in that attitude, I said to myself: 'How good she is! She is like the little madonna in the other room.' After this I was no longer concerned about my brothers but crept back down the stairs. I did not see her around the house for quite some time after that."

Her heart was already devoted, and it was driven on to meditate on God and to seek solitude, as her mother testifies. Her mother told Father Ildephonse on the occasion when he was being shown the little room where the Saint used to go to flee company: "Here, all by herself, my little Anna passed her happiest hours. When I would inquire about her from the servants, they told me that she is always closed up in her room with her holy pictures. If I happened to call her, she would come immediately, but when she had finished whatever I had asked her to do, she immediately returned to the room."

At the age of seven Anna Maria made her first confession, and from that time on she frequented this sacrament "preparing herself for a long time with much compunction." One day her father took her for this reason to the Capuchin church, a short distance from the baronial villa, which was located in a rustic setting. (The family used to spend the summer at this villa; today it is a Discalced Carmelite convent.) On the way home the child, who showed much confidence in her father, spoke about the spiritual life with so much piety and insight that her father was amazed and much comforted.

Did this precocious inclination to the life of prayer contribute toward hastening her parents' decision to place her as a boarder with the Benedictine Sisters in Florence? There is nothing to support this opinion because we know that they sent several other daughters to the same place when they were about this same age; but, whatever the case may be, Anna Maria was pleased by the decision, especially since she had heard that "it was easier to serve God there."

We know for certain that Anna Maria Redi was happy at the convent school.

It would be a mistake to think that the type of life led there was the same as that of a modern boarding-school. At that time, a limited number of girls were admitted into the interior of the cloister. Each of them was assigned to a governess. To the Saint was given Mother Eleanor d'Albizzi who later was to become abbess and who would testify at the beatification process. Her testimony, however, is insignificant because in her eyes Anna Maria was only a good little girl, pious and virtuous indeed, but in no way distinguished from her companions. She remarked in her testimony that others were able to see better than she into the Saint.

I cannot omit a comment of one of the confessors of the abbey, Don Bertini, who was ordinary confessor during the last years Anna Maria spent there. When he was asked what he thought of Anna Maria, he answered (it was the Saint's sister who has preserved his remark for us): "She was a young girl, impertinent like all the others." I must admit that this remark aroused my curiosity. Perhaps it was only a whim on his part, but maybe the Saint was not the sweet little girl that many think she was and that, in cultivating the hidden life, she was only following her natural inclinations.

The documents of the process tell us a great deal about her personality: she was spirited and would have been rather short-tempered if she had not learned from childhood to curb herself. She was very sensitive and felt great repugnances. She managed to overcome them, but the effort in doing so often made her face glow with color. She retained this imperfection to the very last years of her life although her self-mastery, even externally, was complete. Nevertheless, she had to combat her dislikes to the end of her life. We shall see how they manifested themselves in her last years.

We are told more about the last years the Saint spent at Saint Apollina's than the first ones. She was nine years and four months old when she entered. The following year (1757) she made her first Holy Communion and received Confirmation. But it was not until the age of fourteen that we are able to notice a new perspective in her spiritual life.

Since the preceding year, feeling the need for direction and little inclined to manifest herself to her friends—impelled, we might say, by her already intense desire not to make herself noticeable—she began a correspondence with her father. To him she revealed herself with complete confidence, and this profited both of them. There was some discussion about a religious vocation, and Anna wanted to remain with the Benedictines. Being a prudent man, her father, in order to ensure her a free choice, made her return home until she attained the age when, according to the custom of the times, a girl could make her final decision. Anna Maria Redi left Saint Apollina's when she was sixteen years and eight months old (1764).

In 1761 the Saint had made, together with the Benedictine sisters, a retreat preached by the confessor of the house, Dom Dante Pellegrini. He was a priest of deep spirituality; his wonderful manner of speaking renewed Anna Maria's fervor, and this was soon noted by her companions. One of them, Lady Eleanor Prudenziana Bracci, who was particularly friendly with her (and who also testifies that the Saint was very careful at that time to keep her interior life hidden even from the religious), tells us that this retreat was definitely the beginning of new intensity in her spiritual life. The girl could easily talk with the preacher since he was the confessor, but he, being gifted with remarkable insight, was aware of her inclination not to be singular, and, accordingly, he avoided long discussions with her, contenting himself with giving her briefly the direction she needed. Anna Maria supplied whatever was lacking by the correspondence with her father.

Dom Pellegrini taught her the practice of prayer. He gave her a good book of meditations, *Il cibo dell'anima*, which treated of all the fundamental dogmas of the faith with special emphasis upon the Passion of Christ. From that time Anna Maria made a half-hour prayer in the religious' choir each day. Her recollection became more intense.

Her recollection was particularly noted at Communion time. The confessor allowed her to communicate with the same frequency permitted to the religious. During these moments of grace Anna was ordinarily so absorbed that it was often necessary to jostle her in order to remind her that it was time to leave the choir. But she knew how to regain her composure quickly, and so it attracted little attention.

At this point we can notice an increase in her desire of self-oblation and self-immolation. She arose at night to pray—until the indiscretion of her younger sister, Cecilia, who came to join her and who impresses us as being rather undisciplined, betrayed her. Naturally, prohibition followed. At this time she also began to take the discipline, and the religious who secured one for her used to keep guard while she took it. She blushingly told all this later to Father Ildephonse.

We cannot doubt that Anna Maria's spiritual life during this period was centered on Jesus. She adored and loved Him in the Blessed Sacrament. She meditated upon His sacred Passion and acquired a devotion for the images representing it, which was to be a life-long characteristic of the Saint. She sensed the necessity of uniting herself to Our Lord in His Passion by the practice of mortification. All these things, however, occurred in the greatest secrecy, and it was only on occasion that her bearing would betray her deep recollection. All the characteristics of a contemplative soul were already noticeable in her; above all, she was "smitten" by her God: she must love Him.

Is it permissible to date her devotion to the Sacred Heart as being inaugurated at this time?

We feel that we would be correct in doing so. Saint Teresa Margaret already possessed a deep devotion to the Sacred Heart when she arrived at the doors of Saint Teresa's monastery in the September of 1764. It was this devotion which gave rise to her suffix in religion ... "of the Sacred Heart of Jesus." Because this devotion was still rather new, it was not too well received at Saint Apollina's. Nothing can be said about the attitude of Dom Pellegrini toward the devotion, but his successor, Dom Bertini, was openly opposed to it and said that it was "invented by the Jesuits." I sometimes wonder whether or not he discussed this matter with his young penitent, and if a quick response on her part in defense of the devotion might have caused his judgment of her as being "impertinent." Be it as it may, I think that young Anna Maria learned of the devotion from her father. He had a Jesuit brother, Father Diego Redi, who was deeply attached to it and composed hymns in honor of the Sacred Heart. Her father assures us that she learned of the devotion from books of sound doctrine that he himself helped her to obtain, just as he later obtained for her the life of St. Margaret Mary Alacoque. This latter book played a tremendous role in the spiritual development of our Saint, who made Margaret Mary her spiritual "Mistress."

It will suffice for our purpose at the present to recall that devotion to the Sacred Heart is a devotion of love, one which will have us realize that we must return our love in response to the great love of the Divine Heart toward us. This was to become the Saint's motto: "to give love for love." I do not know if she formulated this ideal while she was at Saint Apollina's, but we shall very shortly see that when she left the Benedictine convent school, love had already become the driving force of her life.

The month of September 1763, was to unexpectedly turn her contemplative aspirations toward Carmel.

At this point we are going to discuss an extraordinary favor which is indeed remarkable since it is unique in her life. Saint Teresa Margaret is no saint of revelations. She traveled to the very end of her life in the "naked faith" extolled by Saint John of the Cross. Yet, at the very source of her decision to embrace the austere life of Carmel we find a supernatural "locution." We cannot deny it. Not only is it well substantiated[1] but we even see it reflected in everything she did during the few months separating her from her entrance into Carmel.

In September, 1763 Anna Maria received a parting visit from one of her friends from Arezzo who was entering the Discalced Carmelites. The friend was young Cecilia Albergotti, later Sister Teresa of Jesus Crucified. At the moment of parting, the Saint heard a voice: "I am Teresa of Jesus—I want you among my daughters." Distressed and quite upset, young Anna fled to the choir to the feet of the Eucharistic Christ to Whom she always fled for help. Again she heard: "I am Teresa of Jesus, and I tell you that in a short time you shall be in my monastery."

It is quite evident that the last months spent by the Saint at Saint Apollina's were painful for her. She who had for years cherished the desire of being a nun could no longer bear living in the convent. She said nothing, however, to anyone about what had happened—not even to her father.

The nuns, who were certain that she would join them, remained in suspense, because the Saint said nothing to them about her plans. They were very upset when they later learned of her decision.[2]

Anna Maria returned to the bosom of her family in Arezzo in the April 1764 so that she might "consider at her ease the choice of state in life" as her father wished her to do. No decision was to be announced until her seventeenth birthday, and three months remained until that time. They were to be filled with a life combining piety with a regulated social life. Here we see that her father, who was a very prudent man, wanted her to taste this form of life also, in order that she might be fully aware of her choice. But, deep in the heart of the Saint, the decision had already been made.

We have to admire the prudence of this child who bore in her heart the secret of a word that she believed divine and yet who would never use it to obtain consent for something she so desired. Even though Anna Maria was still a child in years, she was not so spiritually. She was already mistress of herself, of her interior movements as well as those of the exterior. Everything in her was under perfect control and directed only to God. She already possessed great maturity of soul.

The months passed at the paternal home are very revealing. Her mother was sick. It was her father who took her to Church and later on a pilgrimage. She obeyed him simply and without formality, even to the wearing of worldly ornaments that she detested. The hairdresser tells us that she would never look into a mirror when he offered her one. Anna Maria was already too absorbed in God to interest herself in anything except Him. It sometimes happened that while she was with her family she would become very abstracted: "Come back to us, Miss Anna!" her father would jokingly call. And then she would smile. However, when her father would talk with her at night about God she was happiest, for then she was in her element.

He took her to church for confession and communion. She went there only for Jesus; nothing else interested her, and she did not take notice of things. Her father was astonished when, entering the Jesuit church after having come there many times previously, Anna asked him which church this was, as if it were completely new to her.

At home during the day the Saint sought solitude and peace in which to pray. This most assuredly was not an easy thing to do in a house full of little children—there were thirteen in all. The eldest had been sent to boarding-school, but Anna was always surrounded by four or five little noise-makers. She often tried to bribe them: "Now, go out; make no noise and if you will be good you shall have a holy picture." The boys went out, and Anna hid herself behind a screen. The little tricksters would then sneak back in order to watch her. They would find her kneeling on her prie-Dieu, and she would remain a long time in prayer.

Her room was the witness of much prayer and mortification. At night Anna used to remove the mattress in order to sleep upon the bed-frame. She arose early in the morning to put everything in order so that nothing would be noticed.

On her seventeenth birthday (July 15, 1764) Anna told her mother that she wished to be a Carmelite nun. Her father was stunned by his daughter's announcement.

A prudent father, Ignatius Redi wanted to secure all possible assurance for himself and his daughter. He wanted her vocation examined. Beside Father Gioni—the Jesuit who directed her—he wished to have the opinion of some expert in discerning religious vocations. Canon Tonci, who lived in the neighboring city of Castiglione, was asked to perform this task. On three consecutive evenings Anna Maria underwent a long examination. Afterward, the Canon pronounced a favorable judgment.

Who should happen to pass through Arezzo during these days and stay at the Carmelite monastery of Our Lady of Grace? None other than the provincial of the Tuscan province of the Discalced Carmelites, Father John Colombino. He was to become a great friend of Ignatius Redi. He possessed remarkable insight into spiritual matters. His judgment confirmed that of the other two priests: he was certain that Anna Maria was called to be a Carmelite nun.

The Saint's parents were good Christians and now, reassured by such illustrious persons, they were not going to oppose the vocation of their daughter. Application for admission was made at the Florence Carmel. Since she was recommended by the provincial, she was accepted. The month of August had hardly passed when all the arrangements had been decided upon.

Anna Maria wrote to the nuns in Florence telling them that she wished to enter the monastery in order to compete with her companions there to see "who would love God most." She was going to Carmel to realize the dream of her life: to love God, to give Him some return for the immense love that He had shown to her.

It was a local custom in Arezzo that each candidate to the monastic life, before entering the convent, visit the nearby solitude of La Verna where Saint Francis received the stigmata. Anna Maria loved Saint Francis very much, and she had a great desire to make this pilgrimage, but she said nothing of it. What self-mastery we see in this child! Yet she was beside herself with joy and extremely grateful when her father came to the decision (on his own initiative) to take her there.

One of the Apostolic Processes gives us a detailed account of this pilgrimage from an eyewitness. It is a delightful page to read. In complete harmony with everything else we know of the Saint, it shows us how her soul was completely given to God and occupied with

Him. Indeed it was no "beginner" who knocked at the door of the convent on September 1, 1764.

The first impression that the new postulant made upon Sister Anna Maria Piccolomini has been recorded for us. This good nun had the duty of seeing after the needs of the newcomer. She was convinced that the soul of Anna Maria Redi was already totally dedicated to the love of God.

From the very first moment she spent in the Carmelite cloister Anna Maria felt at home. Her virginal purity and ardent love could come to flower only in this convent, the Florence Carmel. Austere and virtuous, the Carmelite nuns awed the newcomer, and she felt great admiration for them. As long as she lived with them the Saint felt herself most unworthy of living under the same roof as these holy creatures. Yet, in spite of this sense of unworthiness, she trembled lest she be sent away when the time of the traditional votation for approval came.

Happiness radiated from her person. Although there was a touch of aristocracy in her, it is all the more beautiful to read how, from her first days in the convent, she practiced real mortification. She disposed of a mattress that had been given her for the first few days by bearing it on her own shoulders to the room of a sick novice, so that this latter might be a little more comfortable. She asked Mother Anna Maria for permission "to fly" (along the paths of holiness) and showed the Reverend Mother a packet of wormwood—of which she already knew the use. A simple gesture was sufficient to make her drink the heavy soup served in the refectory. To the end of her life the little nun was to experience a great repugnance for the plainness of the meals, but since it was to be her ordinary fare, she tried her best to overcome her distaste.

Teresa Margaret was serious about everything she did, and she was very recollected in doing it. This characteristic was noticed by all the Sisters on the very first evening the Saint spent in Carmel. Scarcely had she entered the enclosure when someone told her that she would have an opportunity on the next day to receive Holy Communion and that it was possible for her to go to confession right away. The Saint took advantage of this opportunity and knelt near the confessional to prepare herself for confession. The confessor was told that he should wait for her and wait he did! The community also was waiting for her because they wanted to speak with her. Neither the one nor the other saw any trace of her. Mother Anna Maria went to investigate. She finally found the girl still making her preparation with great recollection. The very same evening a similar incident occurred: she asked permission to make her preparation for Holy Communion, and this time the Mistress had to come and tell her that it was time to retire.

The training received by the new postulant during this period was solid but rather austere. The Mistress was severe and permitted nothing to pass. She allowed no opportunity for humbling the girl slip by. But Anna Maria received it all graciously and even with gratitude.

She was nourished on the purest Carmelite doctrine. She had a special love for Saint Teresa whose works she kept in her cell. It was her custom to look up some little spiritual saying each time that she entered the cell. Saint Teresa was always to be her ideal, her model. Because she had a concrete and very practical mind, Anna Maria developed a special taste for the works on the formation of Carmelites written by Venerable John of Jesus-Mary: *The Instruction of Novices* and *Discipline in the Cloister.* Later she would add *Customs of the Novitiate of Pastrana* to these favorites.

Joy seems to have been the dominant characteristic of Anna Maria during this period. It was the type of joy experienced and expressed by one who has arrived in port after a long journey. In order to consider it, we need only read a letter in verse which she sent her father toward the end of December 1764.

Dalla mia amata cella	From my beloved cell
ove riposo in pace	where I dwell in peace
se pur cosi ti piace	(if one finds it to his liking)
Ti vengo a salutar ...	I am coming to greet you ...
Gran piacere in ver trovai	Truly I have great pleasure
Nell'entrare in monastero	in entering the monastery;
ma il contento fu piu vero	but my joy shall be greater still
quando dentro mi trovai ..	when I find myself really within ...
Deh! permettimi ch'almeno	Permit me at least
io ti dia un caro amplesso	to embrace you with delight
e ti mostri al tempo stesso	and show you at the same time
le gran gioia che ho nel seno ...	the happiness of my heart ...
Cosi ben mi son trovata	I find such great pleasure
di si amabile soggiorno	in this delightful sojourn
Che mi sembra solo un giorno	that it seems only a day
d'esser quivi io dimorata ...	that I have been here ...
Tant 'allegra e si contenta	Never as at present
Come or sono non sono mai stata,	have I been happy and content,
sana sono; ma pur malata	I am well; but sickness nor
il dolor non mi sgomenta.	suffering frightens me.
Mia delizia e sempre stata	My delights will always be
di tener in allegria	to keep joyous
cosi bella compagnia	this wonderful company
e vederla sollevata ...	and to see it rested ...

A contagious joy breaks loose in these strophes where she is telling her father that the period of postulancy is ended and that soon she hopes to receive final permission to be clothed in the holy habit. Throughout the entire poem she reveals herself, and in the last lines especially does her playful humor become apparent. "Sono furbina"— "I am a little imp"—she was to write a priest a few days before her death when she asked him for a poem for a feast that she was preparing as a surprise for her companions. Then she was in complete desolation of soul—but nothing of her natural self had fled her in spite of it. Her self-possession was always admirable.

The verses which we quoted make some illusion to an illness. The truth is that Anna Maria was forced to keep to her bed at the very moment that her postulancy—which at that time lasted three months ordinarily—had terminated. An abscess on her knee, which she had concealed as long as it was possible, caused her a terrific fever and hindered her from moving about. It became necessary to call a surgeon, and it was this event that brought her strength of soul to light. She did not flinch under the scalpel; she considered herself fortunate to be able to immolate herself thus to God.

Anna Maria did not leave the cloister until the end of the fourth month (January 4th to be exact), and then she was hospitalized at the request of her father in the home of Lady Isabella Barbolani Mozzi, a pious widow who lived in Florence. Shortly afterward, Ignatius Redi came to bring her home so that she could make her parting visits to her brothers, sisters, and other acquaintances. At this time two of her sisters (Cecilia and Eleanor) were attending Saint Apollina's, and two of her brothers (Gregory and Francis Xavier) were in the Cicognini College in Prato. This latter brother, Francis Xavier, was the one closest to her. From him we learn of the event that proves once more that the Saint was completely dedicated to the love of God and to the desire of making Him loved.[3]

On the tenth Anna Maria reentered the cloister to begin her novi-tiate. She received the Carmelite habit on the following day.

The separation from her father caused the Saint a real act of heroism. It appears that he possessed less self-control than she. So upset was he after his daughter crossed the threshold of the cloister that he did not dare on the following day to assist at the ceremony; he contented himself with watching it from afar, more or less hidden from the public. The Saint herself was deeply moved. In fact, the separation from her father was one of the greatest sacrifices demanded of the girl in her entire life. She behaved manfully, but she still felt the immediate effects. Mother Anna Maria, who went out of charity to visit her cell after she had retired, found her flushed from the effort she was making to control her feelings. The good Mother told her to give vent to her tears in order that she might be able to relax a little.

In religion Anna Maria Redi took the name Sister Teresa Margaret of the Sacred Heart of Jesus.

Her novitiate was a period spent in exceptional fervor. We know already that the Mistress of Novices spared her nothing. This was what Teresa Margaret wanted, however, because she was "in a hurry" to unite herself with God. The ordinary confessor of the monastery, Father Gregory of Saint Helen, understood this holy impatience, and a few weeks after her investiture, on the feast of Easter, he gave her permission to make her vows privately and to renew them from time to time.

In addition to Father Gregory, Father John Colombino, the provincial who had examined her vocation, continued his interest in her. To him she came about a doubt that she experienced with regard to her vocation. If we might make a judgment from the answer of the priest (which has been preserved for us), it seems that the doubt revolved around the extraordinary manner in which the Saint's vocation was manifested. The good father reassured the little nun and made her see how the doubt was nothing other than a temptation of the devil.

Not many months after she entered the novitiate, Teresa Margaret met the religious who was to become her real director, Father Ildephonse. We do not know the reason behind his taking care of the direction of her soul; perhaps it was because she feared to approach the provincial or maybe he was so burdened with the duties of his office that he was unable to help her. Whatever may have been the cause, this excellent theologian assumed the direction of the Saint until the day of her death. It was either in the end of November or in the beginning of December 1765 that Father Ildephonse took charge.

We do not possess a "journal" that would permit us to follow the progress of the Saint during the year of novitiate, but we do have a document that enables us to measure the progress she made up to the beginning of the new year.

"My Jesus, my Love, I resolve to be Yours, regardless of the repugnance that I might have to face," she wrote with her blood at the beginning of her religious life. Now that she had officially entered into her career, she intended to proceed to the end with complete devotion. The paper which she wrote on the occasion of her profession manifests a soul completely dedicated to the task of conquest— a conquest aimed at making her "all God's."

The paper of which we are speaking is the collection of notes she made during the retreat preceding her solemn vows and which she organized into a whole immediately after the profession. These notes manifest great spiritual depth and, at the same time, a remarkable intellectual insight. St. Teresa Margaret had been in Carmel scarcely eighteen months, months that had been passed in performing household chores; she had received no more than the amount of instruction ordinarily received during the novitiate. Therefore it is a matter of astonishment to see such a young child—only 19—assimilate so completely the spirit of her Order and grasp the significance of its spirituality so well that it exerted great power over her intellect. Not only did Teresa Margaret understand the true meaning of detachment and recollection, the two great instruments of asceticism so vital to Carmelite spirituality, but she even outlined her "plan of conquest" with a logic based upon these two principles.

We are speaking throughout this discussion of a "conquest"; no word seems more fitting to describe the personal effort demanded of the Saint if she intended to comply with the resolutions in her retreat notes. It is a very precious document because it clearly indicates the intimate dispositions of the Saint during this period of her life that we are taking the liberty to call the "ascetical period."

Face-to-face with the end that she was seeking, Teresa Margaret determined to apply herself with even greater courage to a complete "reform of self" than she had done previously, and, wishing to keep it within the Carmelite way of thought, she added: "to detach self completely from all my natural inclinations in order to adhere the better to You, My divine Creator." Teresa Margaret understood that total detachment would free her soul so that it could ascend without hindrance to God, that abnegation would prepare her for a relationship with God in prayer which would gradually become more and more unitive; upon both of these she centered all her attention so that, in their wake, she might obtain some concrete results—for Saint Teresa Margaret was, above all, a highly practical person. Thus, instead of dreaming her life away in the world of ideas and inventions, she went directly to regular monastic observance, knowing that there she would find "the form and mode of life to which You, my Jesus, in Your kindness have called me."

It was her greatest desire that her abnegation be complete, that it extend to all those little attractions which had the power of enslaving her will (which must belong to God alone) by vain complacency and selfish satisfaction. Teresa Margaret, therefore, embraced obedience "total, in everything, prompt," a complete renunciation of self-will; "a more minute mortification of all my attractions, passions and senses" to make all seeking after personal satisfaction die. She cultivated great kindness toward all of her sisters and proposed "to be indulgent with them on all occasions, to hide and excuse their faults, to speak to them with great esteem" so that she might be able to eliminate all severity of judgment and all the demands of self-love. She further resolved to put herself under the feet of all, proposing "to flee and hold in abhorrence all praise and never to say anything that might either directly or indirectly secure praise for me."

Glancing through the abundant testimonials embraced within the process of beatification regarding the heroic virtues of the Saint, we are assured that her resolutions were not merely written on paper and then forgotten, but that they were observed to the letter.

It is not sufficient merely to mortify one's will; we must order our intellectual life also if we wish to be totally occupied with God in continual prayer. That is the reason why Teresa Margaret placed resolutions regarding the purification of the intellect immediately after those treating of the will.

Sister Teresa Margaret, knowing "that a person cannot be all Thine unless she detach her mind and heart from all preoccupation with this world so that her soul will be centered only on Thee," resolved to detach herself from all news that might come to her from outside the convent. But she was aware that this would not suffice of itself; she would have to renounce all that she could learn of the "little world" that was the convent itself because it would only fill her mind with many useless thoughts and anxieties. She resolved, therefore, to be "always silent regarding what my sisters do, deaf to whatever they might say, blind to whatever I might see." Thus did Teresa Margaret plan to mortify her senses in order that they might be free "to serve, praise and bless You, my God and my only good."

All the information given us by the process of beatification regarding her observance of this detailed silence and delicate modesty shows us once again that the resolutions made by Saint Teresa Margaret became genuine rules of conduct. Father Ildephonse assures that, if the Saint ever made a resolution, it became for her the equivalent of a vow, for she was very diligent in putting it into practice.

We can easily see how a life of prayer founded upon virtues generously practiced could very easily become contemplative. In fact, when Father Ildephonse met Sister Teresa Margaret, we are certain that it occurred during the year of novitiate toward the end of 1765—he found her in "the prayer of faith" that is so aptly described by Saint John of the Cross. In this prayer, which, incidentally, belongs to the genera of contemplative prayer, the simplified activity of the soul meets with a divine infusion that, even if it is hidden, can still leave the soul in utter darkness. This was obviously the case with Teresa Margaret who included among her resolutions the desire to be faithful in the "exercise of the presence of God" and coupled with it the desire to be especially faithful "to the hours of prayer prescribed by the Constitutions, never leaving the choir without the blessing of obedience and for a grave reason." Further, she wished to be exact and faithful despite the "aridities, agonies, boredom, and desolation that it might please You to send me, even if it be in the very exercise of prayer."

Here we can surmise that the Saint was far from continual enjoyment of celestial favors. The ordinary climate of her prayer was that of aridity and trial, and we are going to see that this was the case to the end of her life.

At the present, however, we are still concerned with the first phases of her life of prayer that were, thanks to the prayer of faith, leading the Saint into an atmosphere of "passivity." It does not appear that it was "experimental" the majority of the time; God was secretly doing great things in her. Nothing was to astonish her more than the day when the divine action suddenly burst upon her consciousness and flooded over into her entire being.

The document that we are analyzing finishes with a resolution "to conquer valiantly all repugnances that I often feel in manifesting my interior and all my aspirations to the one whom You have chosen to be my spiritual director." We delight in being able to dwell on this "common" characteristic of the spirituality of the Saint and to note that the complete candidness that was the theme of her relationship with her confessor, far from being natural to her, was actually a matter of great repugnance and effort. Yet nothing, regardless of what it might be, regardless of how difficult it was, was going to deter her from uniting herself to the Beloved of her soul.

It is necessary for us to study her prayer a little more.

This period of aridities, of which she speaks, was no longer a part of the first stages in the life of prayer. We know that she exercised herself in prayer from the age of fourteen and that it was not very long before she possessed some facility in recollecting herself. When she entered Carmel, Teresa Margaret was experienced in being able to maintain contact with God.

This prayer of faith, while bearing her to "the lofty contemplation of the divine attributes and perfections," would never separate her from Jesus. Her starting point and mainstay in prayer continued to be "the mysteries of the life, passion, and death—in a word, the human-ity—of Jesus Christ, as well as His maxims and doctrine ...." From

Jesus, the God-Man, Teresa Margaret rose to God and penetrated "contemplatively" into the divine mysteries. Even in this she remains perfectly conformed to the Teresian ideal. Saint Teresa of Jesus was constant in teaching her daughters that, even if they might be elevated to great contemplative heights, they must nevertheless remain attached to Jesus. Teresa Margaret was exact in following this advice.

In her resolutions about abnegation, she returned to Christ as her model. She must imitate Him because "the bride cannot be pleasing to the Bridegroom unless she studies to be as much like Him as possible." For this reason she desired "to be crucified with Him." It was so that she could truly be called His bride that she resolved to "control my predominant passions." It was His image that she sought in her sisters, as she served their needs. It was before Jesus that she wanted to abase herself. To Him she addressed herself when formulating new resolutions, new modes of conduct. Obviously, Jesus was the center of her spiritual life. Later we shall see how He brought her to the holy Trinity Itself.

In her method of practicing the presence of God, Teresa Margaret liked to keep in contact with Our Lord's eucharistic presence. For her the focal point of the convent was the tabernacle, and her imagination and heart constantly carried her there.

We should have a very poor grasp of the spirituality of Saint Teresa Margaret if we were unaware of the role that the Holy Eucharist played in her life—to be truthful, it was the leading role in her life. For her the Eucharistic Jesus was the Jesus Who lived with her and to Whom she turned in everything. She succeeded admirably in having perfect harmony between her life of prayer and her duties in life by seeking in the latter only the Will of God. Yet this Will is the Will of Jesus in the tabernacle; thus, she lost nothing through her occupations and actually drew nearer to Him. During the recitation of the Divine

Office (which in Carmel always takes place near the tabernacle) Teresa Margaret exulted in His presence; she had written the following words on a scrap of paper that she kept before her in her breviary: "Eyes to the earth—heart to God! God is present here!"

Although she lived in an era that had little appreciation for the liturgy, Sister Teresa Margaret, thanks to her knowledge of Latin, nourished herself upon the sacred texts that she penetrated "contemplatively" and that came often to her lips during the day. She assisted "liturgically" at Holy Mass, noting particularly the essential parts[4], trying to arouse dispositions appropriate to the different movements of the holy sacrifice. To sum it up: she united as closely as possible liturgical life to personal piety, a meditative life to a contemplative life. And all this makes us feel her very near us. She was not a saint led by extraordinary ways; she used (just as we do) that great spiritual ensemble that is accessible to each of us, and which modern spirituality teaches us to know and esteem better.

I like, above all, to see her (although a mystic who was to reach the highest levels of the contemplative life) so assiduously diligent in the practice of ascetic virtue—something she tried never to omit. She avoided even the slightest shadow of theoretical and practical quietism. Here we have a true daughter of Saint John of the Cross, in whom contemplative prayer expanded, who was "determined" to embrace "not the easiest but the most difficult; not that which pleases but rather what displeases; not the greater but the lesser ...."

In this period we can also note a deepening of the Saint's devotion to the Sacred Heart. The occasion for this was her father's gift to her of the biography of (the then) venerable Margaret Mary Alacoque. Father Colombino gave her permission to use it. Father Ildephonse is not certain if it occurred during Father Colombino's term as provincial (to May 1766) or during the time he was ordinary confessor of the nuns (to August 1767 when he died). We can, however, assert that she was already using the book when she wrote the notes of this retreat; we base this opinion upon certain expressions that she used.

The life of the Venerable Margaret Mary, written by Msgr. Lenguet, bishop of Soissons, had been published in an Italian version in Venice in 1740. It contained abundant quotations from the writings of the Visitandine nun. Reading through this book Sister Teresa Margaret experienced profound emotion in her soul: here was an ideal realization of the secret aspirations of her own soul. The entire vocation of Margaret Mary to love became concrete in her devotion to the Sacred Heart, and therefore it is not surprising to note that Teresa Margaret made her her "mistress." Nor was this an empty term. The whole mind of Margaret Mary became that of Teresa Margaret's, and the Carmelite nun adopted even the expressions of the Visitandine as her own. There was a complete assimilation; there was nothing present to hinder the union of the special characteristic of our Saint—her tendency to the hidden life—with the spirituality of Margaret Mary—rather, it even favored it. We shall see in a little while how this "fusion" led the Saint to the sublimity of spiritual life in the Trinity. Her spiritual itinerary was truly *from the Sacred Heart to the Trinity*—by passing through the depths of the hidden life.

Father Ildephonse related in a very precise manner the way in which Teresa Margaret conceived devotion to the Sacred Heart. He learned it from her own lips, after he had asked her on several occasions about it. We are quite certain that, from this period until the end of her life, Sister Teresa Margaret did not vary substantially in her concept, but she did become more precise with the passage of time.

The good Father tells us that she considered the Sacred Heart "the center (of manifestation) of the love of the Divine Word, Who loved us from all eternity in the bosom of the Father and Who, thanks to this same love, has obtained for us the ability to love Him in return, both on earth and in heaven, by participating in His love. This is the meaning which ... I find that she gave to this devotion, making it consist completely in loving in return the One Who has first loved us."

It is apparent that, for Teresa Margaret, devotion to the Sacred Heart ascended to the divine, eternal love of the Word, a love manifested in the Sacred Heart, a love whose most precious fruit is to make us capable of loving supernaturally, of repaying this great love by a love of the same order: the love of charity. Practically speaking, therefore, devotion to the Sacred Heart consists in "returning love for love." In fact, this need of "loving in return" was already the entire life of Teresa Margaret, and it grew ever more deeply a part of her.

This need of loving—or rather of "giving love to God," for her love was free from self-interest—manifested itself during this period by the practice of challenges that she took up with her companions in the cloister and even with friends outside the monastery. This is not only a means of stirring up one's own love, but it does more: it procures for God the love of other souls.

The practice of challenges in Carmel can be traced back to Saint Teresa, and they can concern any virtue. For Sister Teresa Margaret they all involved in some way or other the exercise of the love of God.

One of these, addressed to Sister Teresa of the Crucified (Albergotti), reveals much about her devotion to the Sacred Heart. Apparently, the challenge was made during the period of which we are speaking and was intended to last until the end of her life. Sister Teresa Albergotti said that Teresa Margaret never left her a moment of peace, for she was always urging her on to the practice of a more genuine love. We still have about twenty notes that the Saint wrote her companion on this subject; unfortunately, none of them is dated. We can see there how the Saint used the expressions of Venerable Margaret Mary, copied literally from the biography, and how she put them into the mouth of her "mistress." They have not, therefore, any pretension at originality so far as the text is concerned, but they are original in the way the Saint employed them.

If devotion to the Sacred Heart flourished in any way in the Florence Carmel at this time, Saint Teresa Margaret played her part in it. It is she who was responsible for the first celebration of the feast of the Sacred Heart in that community—and it certainly was in a most original way!

The decree permitting the liturgical celebration of the feast of the Sacred Heart was granted to the Carmelite Order in the first months of the year 1767. However, when someone noticed that the feast was assigned to the Friday after the octave of Corpus Christi, it was decided—in order not to confuse the already existing calendar—to postpone the first celebration of the feast until the following year.

Teresa Margaret was pained by this decision. But what was she to do?

At this time she held the office of sacristan. She asked and obtained from Mother Prioress permission to expose a little picture of the Sacred Heart on the small altar in the convent choir. She then took great pains to see that the altar was decorated as beautifully as possible. Then, in the evening, she sought permission to sing some hymns composed in honor of the Sacred Heart by her uncle, the Jesuit Father Diego Redi, in the room adjoining the choir. She invited the other sisters to join her, and seeing they liked the idea, she asked them to bring along whatever musical instruments they were able to play to accompany the singing. Thus, Sister Teresa Margaret arranged and improvised a concert to supply for the refused liturgical celebration.

But we must retrace our steps and go back to the moment of the Saint's profession (March 12, 1766).

Had she already read in the life of Venerable Margaret Mary this beautiful sentence: "Love does not want a divided heart ... it wants all or nothing"? I do not know; but it is certain that in these days of preparation for the taking of her solemn vows, Teresa Margaret felt more than ever before the desire to offer to love "an integral heart." We feel obliged to remark, for the greater glory of this child, who had entered into religion at the tender age of seventeen, that never did she attach herself perceptibly either to a superior or to a companion. There is not the slightest shadow of this in the entire course of her life. She sought to please God alone. For herself she wanted nothing except to pass unnoticed and be accounted as naught.

We know that Teresa Margaret had a very tender affection for her father, a man who was not only the father of her physical body but who was also the father of her soul. He was blessed in her, for he was a man of great virtue.

When Teresa Margaret, on the vigil of her profession, examined herself and saw that there was nothing more that she could renounce in order to belong totally to God, she felt that her dealings with her father were still a trifle too much on the natural level.

She took advantage of a custom prevalent at the Florence Carmel permitting her to send, on the vigil of her profession, a letter not subject to the scrutiny of her superiors. Thus she sent her father the following message: "My dearest father, I detach myself from you, in order to belong wholly to Jesus." Then she explained to him why she decided to no longer have contact with him other than what was purely spiritual or whenever conventual obedience decided. As a substitute for any natural seeking, she suggested a profound spiritual union, with a daily rendezvous "in the Heart of Jesus."

We still have the letter that Ignatius Redi wrote her on this occasion. He completely accepted the proposition of the Saint, knowing what she meant by it. He was convinced that he would lose nothing;

his affection for her would become only the more pure and the more supernaturally intense.

When she received his last visit in 1769, the year before her death, he was accompanied by her younger brother Francis Xavier who was considering entering the Jesuits. At the process of beatification he tells us that, while speaking with his sister a few moments before the departure of her father, he asked Sister Teresa Margaret: "Are you not pained to leave your father and never more to see him?" She answered with a smile: "Do you think I can take back from God the sacrifice I have made to Him?" "Having said that, she arose and went to the grill where her father was seated. A short distance from him she threw herself on her knees and with a very calm expression asked him: 'Would you give me your blessing?' He arose and blessed her with great emotion and sorrow."

She was never to see him again in this life. But each evening, before retiring, she found her father in the Divine Heart and prayed for him. God could not let this generous loving soul wander very long.

Notes

[1]   The fact is reported by Mother Anna Maria Piccolimini, Sister Magdalene Teresa Vecchietti, Sister Teresa Marie Ricasoli, Father Ildephonse, her father, her brother Francis Xavier, and her sister Donna Gertrude. The Saint tried to keep this grace secret and spoke of it only to her Jesuit uncle and, we are inclined to believe, to Father Colombino who examined her vocation, but this latter is not certain. The Saint had great confidence in her uncle and even up to the time of her profession she maintained a correspondence with him free from censorship. She never re-

vealed this grace to Father Ildephonse, deeming it unnecessary to do so. Later, on one occasion, when she was speaking with her companions on the question of religious vocations, she said that she could never doubt hers. Jokingly, one of her companions, Sister Teresa of the Blessed Sacrament (Morelli), asked her if perhaps her vocation resembled that of St. Aloysius Gonzaga who had heard a voice calling him to the Society of Jesus. Teresa Margaret answered nothing but began to blush furiously. The Saint's sister, Donna Maria Gertrude Redi, a nun at Saint Apollina's, learned of the fact from a letter of their Uncle Diego, and she informed the monastery of the Saint about it in two letters, one to Lady Julia Bellarmini who was a Carmelite postulant for some time and the other to Mother Anna Maria Piccolomini.

2   The Saint's sister tells us that the nuns of Saint Apollina's, having learned of the exact hour when Anna Maria was leaving, were so overcome by grief "that they had to do violence to themselves in order to control their emotions, and of this I was a witness."

3   She embraced him, her face aflame, and said: "My little Francis, do you love Our dear Lord? ... O, really love Jesus—if you only knew how beautiful He is, how good He is, how very loveable! ...." It was almost fifty years later that her brother recalled the incident, and he spoke as if it had just happened.

4   Even prior to her entrance into Carmel, the Saint cherished devotion to her namesake, Venerable Teresa Margaret Farnese of the Parma Carmel, and had copied for her own use a type of horarium from the life of the Venerable that had been used by her. The little Saint of Florence did not do things uselessly as we already know; we can judge just how much she used this schedule by the condition the copy is in. Among other things, there is a method of assisting at Mass in this horarium: "At the offertory I must renew

my profession; before elevation the Lord should be asked to change me into Himself, just as the bread and wine will be; at the elevation itself it is time to adore and again renew the profession, and then to seek from Him whatever my needs might be ...."

PART II

The Mystical Period

During the little Chapter read at Terce on all the Sundays after the Epiphany and Pentecost, the following words from the first epistle of Saint John were chanted: "God is love, and he who dwells in love dwells in God and God in him."

In 1767, probably toward the end of January, while Sister Teresa Margaret was assisting at the recitation of the Divine Office, she was seized with a type of rapture when she heard these words recited by the Hebdomadary.[1] It was so profound that its effects could still be noticed about three days later. Although Teresa Margaret was extremely diligent in hiding the secrets of her interior life, this time she was so overwhelmed by the divine action that she could not detach herself from it. She went through the cloister so elated that she seemed to disregard her natural carefulness regarding the hidden life. Frequently, she repeated the words "God is love" to herself. Others heard her and, wondering about this peculiar behavior, asked her why she repeated these words so often. The Saint, realizing that she had betrayed herself, said: "Having heard them one Sunday at the little Chapter of Terce, I found such sweetness in them, and they made such an impression on me that I feel that I must repeat them."

Sister Teresa Maria Ricasoli, her companion in the novitiate, reports that "Her face was flushed and her bearing was that of one beside himself"; she would pronounce the words "with feeling, in a high voice, with meaning."

Father Ildephonse, who reports that the fact had been told to him by several religious of the monastery, adds that in the choir "she was so enraptured by the words that she remained in a state of elation for

43

several days, during which she often repeated the words to herself quietly ... and, observing the manner and frequency with which she uttered them, one could surmise that they had been accompanied by an extraordinary outpouring of God upon her soul. From that day it was obvious that she was making giant strides forward in the practice of the virtues."

We cannot reasonably doubt that a mystical grace that can produce such psychological and moral effects can belong to the category of unitive contemplation spoken of by Saint Teresa in the fifth and sixth mansions and by Saint John of the Cross in the twenty-sixth stanza of the *Spiritual Canticle*. It is easy to see that, in that moment when she received this grace, Teresa Margaret had "drunk in the interior cellar" spoken of by Saint John of the Cross; furthermore, after the happening itself had passed, she lived in oblivion of everything else and in absorption with God, thus beginning a new stage of the spiritual life.

This indication of unitive grace is not, however, the only one that we have. We find far more convincing proofs in the characteristic sufferings of love that were, at that moment, born in the heart of the Saint and in the interpretation of the words that the Saint herself was one day to give to Father Ildephonse.

He tells us that, when their conversation turned to the love of God, "she began to get rather excited, on one occasion manifesting it by sighs, on another by exclamations sprinkled into the conversation, and still another time by a long discourse in which she made me understand, without intending it, some wonderful concepts of the knowledge and love of God that she had been nourishing in her soul." One day, while he was explaining to her the words "God is love ...", "she told me about divine things, remarking that this charity is the same love with which God loves Himself from all eternity, the Spirit of God Himself, Which is His life and His breath, Who is the Holy Spirit, the Third Person of the Blessed Trinity. And when it is said that he who dwells in charity dwells in God and God in him, the meaning is that he lives in the life of God and God, after a certain fashion, lives His life in him. She concluded: 'thus it is because between them there is but one life, one charity, one God; in God this is all by essence but in the creature by participation and grace; thus it is true that everything is held in common by lovers.'"

A little meditation upon this text will show us that Teresa Margaret must have experimentally known, a state similar to the one described by Saint John of the Cross in the *Spiritual Canticle*. He shows how the soul, mystically transformed in the Holy Spirit, tries to return an equal love to God. If the soul is able to do this, it is because, thanks to the transformation of love, "the soul loves God with the Will of God—which is her will also; thus, she loves God as much as He loves her. The reason for this is that she loves Him with the Will of God and the same love with which he loves Himself—He Who is the Holy Spirit given to the soul."

Teresa Margaret had no other way of learning these lofty secrets of the spiritual life except through her own experience. Experimentally, she knew that divine love (the Holy Spirit invading the soul) is a divine force that embraces and penetrates. It is because she felt within herself the beating of divine love that the little Saint was able to say: he who dwells in love, simply because he is "captured" by love, feels himself to be in God, "lives in the life of God," and he likewise feels that "God, after a certain fashion, lives His life in him." The soul in this state, moved in its depths by the Holy Spirit, feels very vividly His loving embrace, but it feels even more—that it is being carried to God by a movement of love whose strength far surpasses that of the soul. It is a divine strength that elevates it and sweeps it into its current.

The soul, penetrated in this way, feels that it participates in the divine life, that divine love has, in a fashion, become its possession, that it loves "with the Holy Spirit," that "everything is in common," and, above all, that "the love is mutual between the lovers," who are God and the soul.

It would be a very difficult thing to try to assert that in the beginning of the year 1767 Teresa Margaret realized the full import of the grace she had received. All the more reason to doubt the possibility of her full knowledge of the matter is the fact that she said nothing of this supposed knowledge to Father Ildephonse, nor did she tell him of the action of God in her soul when she was making her commentary on "God is love." She did know, however, that, in the very moment when the rapture seized her, she felt herself to be truly loved by God and that she loved God in a divine manner.

Our greatest proof of what happened is the suffering of love that was born in her soul at that moment and that continued to increase until the day she died. Father Ildephonse tells us regarding this matter: "the Servant of God loved, yet she thought that she did not, and from this, experienced tremendous sorrow." This, he says, "became so intolerable ... from the year 1767, particularly from the time when she experienced the long rapture—and grew so much during the last two years of her life that she seemed to me to participate ... in the terrible agony of the Apostle who cried out: 'I desire to be dissolved and to be with Christ.'"

This agony of love explains itself. At the very moment of the unitive rapture, the Saint felt herself to be divinely loved, and she felt that she was able to love God in the same measure in return; but then, as is to be expected, the rapture passed and so did the quickening of love, and she felt herself growing indigent. She was able to remember how much God loved her, but no longer feeling herself to be in "the divine current," she realized how incapable of loving she was. Teresa Margaret found (or at least thought so) that she was not living up to her ideal of love.

We know from what was said earlier that Teresa Margaret dreamed only of "returning love for love." Up to now it had been her devotion to the Sacred Heart that had nourished this ideal in her heart. But it is one thing to know theoretically that one must strive to render God an equal measure of love and quite another thing to feel "experientially" that one is "loved divinely and loves God divinely!" We must remark upon the fact that the grace of "God is love" carried the ideal of Saint Teresa Margaret from the conceptional order to the experiential and mystical order. Until now she had thrown herself toward God to love Him, but now we see in her an invasion of love that was to continually grow more complete in her. It was to awaken in her an unlimited need of loving.

At the present moment, we are at the first step of the mystical period of the Saint; we are at the period when a divine blow unchained an irresistible passion of love in her. Apparently the Saint felt herself introduced into a new world, and she needed some reassurance on what had occurred within her. She, therefore, communicated with her Jesuit uncle, Father Diego Redi. Sister Teresa Maria Ricasoli thinks that the Saint did this with the special intention of finding some way to hide and avoid any exterior manifestation of what had happened within her. It is fortunate for us that the response of Father Diego has been preserved. In it he tries to make her understand that such transports of love ordinarily occur quite frequently in the first steps. Teresa Margaret had expressed her astonishment at the fact that they persisted in spite of what she called "my failings and my ingratitude." The priest reassured her: "your failings ought to root you in profound humility and complete confidence," but he adds, "second the movements of this divine force and make them ever greater by your works."

Obviously, Teresa Margaret experienced a period of frequent transports, but it was not long before she began to know aridity. Now, more than ever before, she began to suffer from not loving.

She had spoken of this pain to the convent's ordinary confessor who, since the summer of 1766, had been Father Colombino. It was he who had given her to the care of Father Ildephonse. Teresa Margaret was delighted to find that Father Colombino was to be her habitual confessor, and he received her confidences on this unique pain that had begun in her soul and that was ever on the increase: the pain of not loving God that she was constantly feeling more and more to be a duty as well as a desire.

Once again we have the answer of the priest recorded for us. It is dated March 31, 1767, and is invaluable in aiding us to establish the chronology of the Saint's spiritual itinerary. The letter is an admirable specimen of spiritual direction wherein the father clearly shows that he holds the upper hand (i.e., that he is the director and not the directed—an easy error for directors to fall into when confronted with privileged souls). We also feel that the father, assured of the Saint's humility, is not afraid to admit the work of God in her soul, and he admits his awareness of her need of comfort. He writes: "... regarding the fact that you feel things to be obscure and yourself devoid of all sentiments, I say, just as I have always held in the matter, that the pain you are experiencing, rising from the desire that burns within you and that is nothing else than love itself, is the daughter of this same love and will actually aid you in attaining a stronger and purer love. This favor you will owe to the pure, yet dry, faith that must sustain you in your accomplishment of the obligation to prayer and the sacraments. The more this will cost you in strength and violence to self ... so much the more will it profit you toward the end that I have already indicated."

When Teresa Margaret received this letter, she was doubtlessly much comforted. To understand that her desire to love was paradoxically making her fear that she did not love removed a heavy burden from her heart and was very reassuring. We can prove this statement by a poem that is attributed to this period and reflects the advice that she had received from her spiritual director.

"Elpina pastorella
calda d'un bel desio
di saper come Iddio
si puote in terra amar,
soletta un di piangea
e nel bosco facea
queste voci sonar:

"Deh! chi mi insegna come
s'ami quel Nume amante,
il qual, pria d'ogni istante
del mondo che creo
con quel medesimo amore
del suo Divino Cuore
anco me stessa amo ...

"Mentre cosi dolente
seco stessa piangeva
ne consolar sapeva
l'interno suo dolor,
la vergine romita
svenne e cadde sua vita
in braccio d'un languor ...

"Ecco, che allor davanti,
adorno d'auree penne,

"Elpina the shepherdess
    burning with a great desire
to know how God
could be loved upon earth,
wept alone one day
and in the woods
uttered these words:

"Eh! who can teach me
to love God Who loves me
and Who, before the existence
of the world He created
with this same love
of His Heart Divine,
loved me...

"While thus grieved
she wept to herself
not being able to console
the pain of her heart;
the virgin, now a hermit,
swooned and fell
a prey to languor ...

"Behold, there before
her, ornate with gilded wings,

dal Cielo ratto ne venne	brimming with celestial delight,
spirto leggiadro si,	stood suddenly a gracious spirit,
che sue belle amorose	and his loving lips
labbra di gigli e rose	like lilies and roses
in questi accenti apri:	opened into these beautiful accents:

Elpina, e come dici	Elpina, how can you say
Non saper amar Dio,	You do not love God,
quando tuo bel desio,	When your very desire
d'amarlo egl'e l'amor?	of loving is love itself?
Egli e la fiamma queta	It is the sweet flame
ch'esce dalla secreta	which escapes from
fornace del tuo cuor ..."	the secret furnace of your heart ..."

Teresa Margaret felt a little comfort in this reassuring answer, but calm did not last long. Although her intellect was satisfied with the knowledge imparted by the letter, her heart was not because it aspired to a greater love. The pain had to return.

The next year (1768) it appears that the Saint was suffering from this same spiritual malady when, upon the approach of her profession anniversary, she made another retreat.

The one who gave this retreat was the ordinary confessor of the monastery, Father John of the Cross, who had succeeded Father Colombino upon his sudden death in the August 1767. Deeply affected by news of the death of this beloved confessor, the Saint accepted it with serenity and was balanced enough in her emotions to be able to console some of the other sisters who seemed to take this untimely death too grievously. They considered the loss irreparable, but Teresa Margaret told them: "We are in the hands of our God Who is the Father of all consolation; whatever happens He permits for our greater good although we may not see this at first. Let's put all our hope in Him. Things will not turn out as you fear because the One

Who could give such excellent qualities to the dead can certainly give them to his successor. According to the degree of the confidence that we put in God will our private spiritual lives and observance grow."

Teresa Margaret spoke well, for the new confessor was also a true servant of God. He understood her spiritual state and aided her very much at a certain time when the devil was trying to trouble her with scruples. Thanks to his excellent gift of observation and energy, the priest managed to eliminate the scruples promptly, and in his action he was very much aided by the docility of the nun.

This confessor testified that the retreat of 1768 marked a new advance in the life of the Saint. Father Ildephonse confirms this observation, and the other nuns, in their turn, marked great progress in the Saint. She became more detached from herself and accepted with admirable serenity the frequent interruptions that intruded into her spiritual exercises. The interruptions had their source in her office as infirmarian, an office that rested completely upon her shoulders at this time.

Once again we have the notes written by the Saint during her retreat. They are far more beautiful than those of her profession retreat. Further, and this is to be noted, they have a very different character. The notes made in 1766 reveal a plan of conquest that had a principally ascetic character; these, on the contrary, show us a soul already moved by the divine power and that, completely convinced of its own utter helplessness, invokes divine assistance to the extent of suggesting a type of madness.

Teresa Margaret presented this sublime page to her confessor at the end of the retreat, and he expressed his approval by adding a Latin text to the end of the page. The flight of soul described by these lines reminds us of the contemplations that the ancients customarily called "circular" from analogy to the circles made by the eagle in his spiral ascent to the sun.

The soul of Teresa Margaret, aware of nothing save God, seems several times to throw itself toward Him with an intense movement of love, yet, each time that it comes to the peak of the movement, the Saint becomes confused at her own total indigence. Thence arises a petition for divine assistance. Then, very suddenly, in the midst of these repeated ascents, we find an "act of oblation."

At first sight this oblation recalls the one made by St. Thérèse of Lisieux about two years before her death. By a curious coincidence this oblation is also found after a long exposition of the sentiments animating the person. All Thérèse's sentiments might be succinctly stated as "wishing to be a saint." But, conscious of her powerlessness and certain that God will never fail her, Thérèse of Lisieux sought an outpouring of merciful love that would sanctify her by consuming her, by transforming her. "In order that my life may be an act of perfect love"— the end desired by Thérèse—"I offer myself as a victim of holocaust to Your merciful love, begging You to consume me without cease"—the means employed to bear her to her end: oblation of self to this overwhelming floodtide of love that seeks to transform the soul. Herein we have also the characteristic insight of Thérèse: she understood that God is love, Who wishes us to leave our misery behind and open ourselves to a "flood of infinite tenderness pent up in Him."

One hundred and twenty-seven years earlier, Teresa Margaret, desiring like Thérèse to "live a life of love," aware of her own helplessness, convinced like her French sister that God is filled with loving goodness toward us, offered herself to the flames of consuming love. She likewise stated that her end is to arrive at the perfection of love but, rather than express it as the Saint of Lisieux did with a slightly abstract formula, Teresa Margaret sought to participate as much as possible in the love of the Heart of Jesus.

Teresa Margaret delighted in considering Jesus her model but, whereas she formerly studied His external acts so that she might imitate Him, she now turned most of her attention to the hidden life of the *soul* of Jesus. There she discovered an intense life of love, so intense that it drove Jesus to a complete holocaust of Himself for His Father's glory and for the good of our souls. She desired to participate as much as possible in this life. "Yes, my God, I do not want anything else other than to become a perfect image of You and, because Your life was a hidden life of humiliation, love, and sacrifice, I desire the same for myself. I wish, therefore, to enclose myself in Your loving Heart as in a desert in order to live in You, with You, and for You this hidden life of love and sacrifice."

To arrive at this goal, Teresa Margaret offered herself to love in terms that anticipate, almost exactly, those of the Little Flower: "You know indeed that I desire to be a victim of Your Sacred Heart, completely consumed as a holocaust by the fire of Your holy love."

Thérèse put her offering under the standard of merciful love; Teresa Margaret placed hers under the banner of the Sacred Heart devotion: "And thus Your Heart will be the altar upon which I must be consumed, my dearest Spouse; You will Yourself be the priest Who must consume this victim by the fire of Your holy love."

The wording here reminds us of the encyclical *Mystici Corporis* that shows us the Holy Spirit, the divine "consuming Fire," inhabiting the soul of Jesus "as His chosen Temple," "procured" for our souls by the merits of the sacrifice that Christ the High Priest offered upon the cross and sent into our hearts by the Incarnate Word, so that this Spirit might make us ever more like Himself. It appears that Teresa Margaret was "before the letter" and had an intuition of the doctrine exposed by Pope Pius XII when she begged Jesus the Priest to consume her with the fire of His Sacred Heart, inhabited by the Holy Spirit and in which He exercised His activity most perfectly.

The oblation terminated in an act of humility combined with great confidence: "How confused I feel to see how blameworthy this victim is, O my God, and how unworthy to be accepted by You as a sacrifice; I feel confident, however, that everything will be reduced into ashes by this divine fire."

Thérèse of Lisieux had conceived the purification of the soul as a primary effect of the overflowing of love into the soul: "at each instant this Merciful Love renews, purifies, and leaves in me no trace of sin." Here again the two Saints agree.

The Little Flower felt that this overflowing of love into her soul would constitute a real martyrdom and described it in the eleventh chapter of her autobiography. Teresa Margaret, once again, parallels the thought of the Little Flower; she too desired to be a victim of consuming love, martyred by this same love.

It suffices to read the document in its entirety (i.e., the act of oblation) to see that Teresa Margaret was obsessed with a longing to love God with the purest and most effective love possible. "I do not propose, O my God, to have any other motive in any of my actions, whether they be exterior or interior, than love alone; I shall check myself in this constantly by recalling that I must strive to return love for love." Apparently here she referred to the care that she would take to acquire pure love. She realized that she could attain it only by God's working within her: "I abandon myself completely to You so that You alone work in me according to Your designs: there is nothing that I want except what You want." Later on, she felt that she must repeat this abandonment once more: "I have abandoned my free will to You so that henceforth You alone will be the possessor of my heart and Your holy Will the rule of my actions."

Could one have better expressed the ideal of transformation of love formulated by Saint John of the Cross: "the state of divine union consists in having the will completely transformed into the Will of God in such a way that it desires naught but what the Divine Will desires, but that each movement be according to the movements of the Divine Will." Further on Saint John writes: "God then possesses the powers as the absolute Lord by their transformation into Him; it is He Who uses them and commands them according to His Spirit and according to His Holy Will."

This is an obvious description of the state that Saint Teresa Margaret had in mind; this was the goal she desired by requesting the invasion of consuming love. Once again she repeated her ideal: "I desire to love You with a patient love, a love dead to self—that is, a love which completely abandons me to You—an active love—to sum it all up, a solid love with no division within itself and which will stand regardless of what may happen."

Now we are going to witness the mystical ascent of the Saint, an ascent that would attain the most sublime peaks, both in the order of knowledge and of love. Never shall we see her enter the extraordinary or charismatic order; yet she arrived at the loftiest heights regardless of this lack. Teresa Margaret reveals herself to us as a "Trinitarian" soul, one whose devotion to the Sacred Heart served as a gateway to the *Sancta Sanctorum* of the spiritual life.

It is remarkable that the mystical ascent of the Saint occurred within a "climate of sorrow." Even at the moment that we think was the time of her arrival at the union of total transformation which, in the language of the mystics, is called the "spiritual marriage," she lived within the shadow of the cross. I like to stress this point in order to make it better understood that it is false to think that this exalted state is free from suffering.

We are going to speak, first of all, about the progress of the Saint in contemplation; second, we shall study the phases of her progress in mystic love. The testimony of Father Ildephonse will assume capital importance because, in the last year of her life, he was her only confidant.

After Father John of the Cross had completed the term of office begun by Father Colombino as ordinary confessor of the convent, he was replaced by Father Valerian, to whom the Saint said nothing about her current spiritual trials. She did this at the advice of Father Ildephonse. Father Valerian, therefore, who was a witness at the process, tells us very little of importance about the Saint. Father John of the Cross, on the other hand, would have been a valuable witness at the informative process; we regret his premature death. Only Father Ildephonse can bear witness to her interior life during this period, but we are certain that he is completely reliable.

When speaking of the contemplation of the Saint, Father Ildephonse remarked that "she bathed in it sweetly to such a degree that, during the last years of her life, it became for her the bitter spiritual agony which it is accustomed to become in souls most advanced in it. To illustrate by using a weak comparison: it is as if a person found himself in an open field during the heat of a scorching summer day; her eyes are so illumined by the light of the sun that, if she were to look at the sun itself, she would see only darkness. This comparison is certainly far from adequate in fully expressing the supernatural effects of divine grace in souls especially dear to God. It is true, nevertheless, that the more the Servant of God was animated and illumined by this elevated knowledge of God, so much the more did it seem to her that she was in a dark forest and in the most parched spiritual aridity. In her knowledge of God, Teresa Margaret no longer knew Him by means of created images but in His perfections themselves; this knowledge poured over into the silence of her faculties and of her heart and, she knew that, regardless of how much she might know of Him in this life—even in purest faith—she still would be far from the Being Who is infinitely perfect and yet supremely simple. So a double pain followed: that of not truly knowing this God (although she did know Him in such a wonderful manner) and that of not loving Him (although she loved Him with her complete being)."

Father Ildephonse is doubtlessly thinking of the *Spiritual Canticle* of Saint John of the Cross which, since 1748, he would have been able to secure in an Italian edition published in Venice translated by Father Mark of Saint Francis. In the commentary on these words of the thirty-ninth strophe:

"on a serene night

with a flame which consumes without giving pain"

we find the inspiration for Father Ildephonse's excellent description.

Contemplation of the most elevated mystical degree always remains a "ray of darkness": "high as this knowledge might be, it still remains a fact that the soul is living in a dark night in comparison with beatific knowledge...." And to live unsated can only be a tremendous pain for a soul desirous of perfect knowledge and deepest love.

It appears that, while remaining within the orbit of terrestrial contemplation, Teresa Margaret had, in the last years of her life, aspired to that ultimate perfection of contemplative knowledge that can be found only in an experience of the mystery of the Holy Trinity.

We have noticed, in studying the notes of her retreat of 1768, that the Saint was strongly attracted to the mystery of the hidden life of Christ. Actually, she was completely dedicated to the pursuit of the life of love that, although hidden, burned in the heart and soul of the Redeemer, and she longed to penetrate into the deepest recesses of this sanctuary so that she might share in that life to the fullest possible degree. But to the interior, hidden life of Christ belongs not only His life of love but also the life of knowledge; thus, after having centered her attention upon the affective aspect of His life, Saint Teresa Margaret now contemplated its intellectual aspect. In all this she burned with the desire of partaking to the greatest possible degree in the activity of this knowledge. We know that the human intellect of Christ, enriched with the light of glory, contemplates the most Holy Trinity with no shadow to obstruct it: It knew that the Person of the Word was the subject of all its human activity; it knew the Father of Whom Christ proclaimed Himself the Son; it knew the Holy Spirit Who resided in His soul "as in His chosen temple" and Who governed all His operations. The spiritual life of Christ was truly "Trinitarian." Teresa Margaret had the desire "to become His perfect image," and in these last years, especially after she had made her act of oblation, she felt a growing need to enter into closest union with the most Holy Trinity.

Father Ildephonse reported that "during the following two years, that is, during the last two years of her life, she asked my permission to imitate the hidden life of Our Savior. When I granted her this permission the first time, I was thinking rather of her exterior life, devoid of any manifestation of what might win the esteem of men. This was my ordinary way of dealing with her. I always let her think that whatever she told me was an ordinary thing and not as lofty as it really was. This did not prevent me, however, from giving her in an indirect manner advice or counsel that she needed. I acted thus to prevent her from having to undergo temptations to vanity. I knew, furthermore, that these words which I spoke, apparently inadvertent and unintended, were far more profitable to her than long discourses. Thus I acted, pretending that I understood her as speaking of the hidden exterior life of Our Lord. During the next year, with more insistence and greater precision, she asked the permission of me once again, recalling to my memory with a touching and tactful modesty everything that she had told me previously. She said that exterior human cares, whether hers or others, had not bothered her at all, thanks to God. To her they were as if they were not. The only thing in this life, she continued, that was worth getting excited about was God and the soul. Then, as I now recall, I began to explain to her the life of Christ, mystically hidden, in a commentary on the words of the Apostle Paul: 'You are dead, and your life is hidden with Christ in God.'"

"She told me that this time I had fully answered the question that she had previously asked of me and that she was able to penetrate more profoundly into the ascetic and mystical implications of the Apostle's words. She then proceeded to harmonize them with other quotations, principally the words of the Savior Himself: 'No one comes to the Father except through Me—who sees Me sees My Father—the just man lives by faith.' It was then that I understood that she was called to emulate this aspect of the Savior's life in faith as far as it is permitted to a creature, namely, the life and the internal, hidden operations of the intellect and will (i.e., the sublime knowledge and affections) of the holy Humanity of Jesus Christ hypostatically united to the Word. Then, with more feeling than she had ever exhibited on any previous occasion, she repeated these words (or their equivalent): 'O Father! What a wonderful ladder is our good Jesus! What a precious and untouchable ladder!' What she intended to say was 'indispensable.'"

In spite of its rather confused style, this page of Father Ildephonse is quite remarkable and reveals the mysterious workings in her soul during the last two years of her life: "She was called to imitate in faith, as far as it is permitted to a creature, the life and the internal, hidden operations of the intellect and will of the Sacred Humanity of Christ hypostatically united to the Word."

Since Christ's intellect, illumined by the light of glory, was completely centered upon the holy Trinity and since Saint Teresa Margaret sought to imitate its intimate, hidden operations, she was necessarily going to become a "Trinitarian" soul.

At this point we must study Teresa Margaret's relationship to the mystery of the Divine indwelling. Whenever she spoke of it with her spiritual director, she used to refer to the beautiful text of Scripture that reveals it to us: "If anyone loves Me, He will keep My word, and My Father will love Him, and We shall come to make our dwelling in him." Then, says Father Ildephonse, "she was all the more intensely taken up with the idea, seized with admiration, wondering at the tenderness of a God Who would deign to make with men a pact of love and friendship that was so unequal."

The indwelling of the blessed Trinity in the soul so touched Saint Teresa Margaret that she used to repeat with great joy the words of the Apostle: "The temple of God, which you are, is holy. For you *are* the temples of the living God as the Lord has said: 'I shall live in them and walk amongst them.'" Another quotation that delighted her was the following from the Gospel: "The kingdom of God is within you." Confronted with such singular richness of the soul she cried: "Oh, what a temple filled with such grandeur! How beautiful is the royal home of our God!"

Here we see how she entwines the thought of the divine indwelling with that of "God is love." We have already seen how Teresa Margaret had been permitted to enjoy the privilege of "feeling experientially" the presence of the God of love in the soul. Father Ildephonse recalled that the feast of the Holy Trinity "was each year for her a day of highest contemplation of this incomprehensible mystery and the day on which she expressed most vehemently her desires of someday contemplating this august mystery in heaven. I recall that the days which she spent in preparation for the feast were as filled with graces as was the feast itself, for she felt within herself tremendous drives toward union with God in the celestial fatherland...they drove her with such force that she often cried: 'When shall I come and appear before Thy Face?'—I also recall one occasion, similar to this, upon which, seized by a rapture, she told me very lofty facts about this mystery, about the relative and eternal operations of the Divine Persons among Themselves. I am forced to admit that I was beside myself with astonishment and admiration." Unfortunately, Father Ildephonse did not desire to go into a fuller explanation of this fact; it would have been highly interesting. In any event, let it suffice for us to say that Saint Teresa Margaret certainly knew mystical Trinitarian contemplation.

We must note that her "life with the Trinity" was not reduced to the mystical manifestation; this came as the crowning point of a long, arduous personal effort to keep herself in contact with this mystery by use of scriptural texts. She assimilated their content by reflective meditation and contemplation of them, which was occasionally rewarded by some mystical grace. Father Ildephonse remarked that the Saint had many personal practices that frequently made her soul rise to the mystery of the Trinity during the day. These practices were based upon the dogma of the Trinity. "She was very devoted to the sovereign mystery of the Holy Trinity which she adored within her heart hundreds of times during the day by using the words: 'Gloria Tibi Trinitas' (Glory be to Thee, Trinity). She often would repeat the words of the elect in heaven: 'Sanctus, sanctus, sanctus Dominus Deus Sabaoth' (Holy, holy, holy Lord God of Hosts). Still again she would use the formula of the Servant of God, Sister Eleanor Ramirez de Montalve: 'Love, praise, honor, glory, thanksgiving be to Thee, most holy, most blessed, most glorious Trinity, one God.' She was accustomed to renewing these acts of adoration in the monastery choir where, as I mentioned previously, she pictured herself in the midst of the blessed spirits. She did this especially when the 'Gloria Patri' and the last strophes of the hymns were said, and in a general way, she wanted to do this at each breath and each beat of her heart, both day and night. Sunday was the day of the week that she set aside in a special manner for honoring the Blessed Trinity with more intense acts of adoration, praise, honor, and gratitude for all the benefits received from the Divine Persons distinct in the unity of God. She was accustomed to honor those perfections that, although common to the members of the Trinity, we mortals are inclined to attribute to each of the Persons separately: omnipotence to the Father, wisdom to the Son, love to the Holy Spirit. Before the throne of the Trinity she would renew all her more particular offerings and vows as if she had only begun to live in that day.

"She celebrated, with all possible solemnity, the feast of the august Trinity that the universal Church celebrates on the Sunday following the feast of Pentecost, and she used to prepare herself for it under my direction and in complete obedience to me by a seven day preparation consisting of various acts of virtue, mortification, internal, and external piety...."

We can conclude from all this that the Saint neglected no means of "living with the Trinity." She was deservedly rewarded by God, therefore, when He permitted her a contemplative glimpse into that mystery.

We can easily surmise the manner in which Saint Teresa Margaret bore herself toward each of the Divine Persons from the testimony in the processes.

Mother Anna Maria Piccolomini tells us: "[One day] she told me that the words 'No one comes to the Father except through Me' always impressed her very deeply; after a few moments she said: 'In this, God the Father is everything, for God is love and has produced all things as an effect of His love! He is the first principle of all things, and this love is God Himself. To conquer Him in Whom is all good, no suffering should seem hard to us, and never must we turn back on account of the difficulties that we might encounter, but rather embrace bitterness and every other type of cross very promptly...."

Mother Anna Maria insisted that these words approximate those of the Saint. They show how she considered the heavenly Father the source of all good Who deserves man's total dedication of himself. She felt deep gratitude to Him for all the gifts that He had so lavishly bestowed upon her. Father Ildephonse remarked: "Her gratitude was very tender, and she frequently had the words of the psalmist on her lips: 'What shall I return unto the Lord for all the things that He has rendered unto me?' or 'Bless the Lord, O my soul, and never forget all the good things you have received from Him.' She would often call upon all creatures: 'Come, listen, and I shall tell to all those who fear the Lord how much He has done for my soul....' She begged me with great humility to unite myself to Jesus and Mary and all the celestial court, particularly during the Holy Sacrifice of the Mass, in order to supplement the gratitude which she felt that she owed to God."

The knowledge that we already have from Father Ildephonse about her contemplation of the relationship between the three divine Persons in the Trinity will show how she considered the Word in the bosom of the Father. She always began with Christ, and she was inclined to view Him as man and as the only way to the Father.

But Teresa Margaret would not have been a Trinitarian soul if she had had no devotion to the Holy Spirit. This phase of her spiritual life is remarkable, and we see her once again uniting herself to liturgical and dogmatic tradition, enlightened with special insights.

Let us recall how she interpreted "God is love, and who dwells in love dwells in God...." She understood by this phrase the experimental and mystical invasion of the soul by the Holy Spirit. Once again we find practices that gave a concrete form to her devotion toward the Spirit of Love whom she honored especially on Pentecost and during the novena in preparation for it. Father Ildephonse observed that "each year on this solemnity she would receive an increase of love for God and of perfection in all the other virtues."

Teresa Margaret considered the Holy Spirit "the source and the substantial life (she meant *stimulus*) of holy love with which she was inflamed and with which she ever desired to burn.... Several times a day she would approach Him in all confidence, humbly begging Him never to be inactive in her heart but rather illumine and increase her love." This devotion of the Saint to the Holy Spirit, the Spirit of Love, permits us to penetrate into another aspect of particular interest in her truly remarkable life: its apostolic aspect.

The ardent desires of the apostolate, the need of procuring in the most efficacious manner the good of the Church, could not fail to have been present in this true daughter of Saint Teresa of Jesus. Teresa Margaret knew that the apostolic means par excellence of the Carmelite soul is intercessory prayer arising from the soul of one dear to God in charity, but she used this intercessory power to try to expand in the Church this wonderful flood of love that she had herself experienced. It seems that she had a profound grasp or intuition of the role of the Holy Spirit in the life of the Church, a role that the tradition of the Holy Fathers, confirmed by the encyclical *Mystici Corporis*, expresses in the adage: "The Holy Spirit is the soul of the Church." Saint Teresa Margaret called upon Him incessantly, begging Him to give to each soul according to its own character that form of spiritual life most necessary for it. Father Ildephonse says: "In her daily prayers she addressed herself to Him on behalf of sinners who had driven Him from their hearts by sin, asking Him to call them back to Himself by strong impulses of grace; she begged for souls tepid in their love, who saddened Him Who dwelt in their hearts by their frequent venial sins, that He would enflame them and make them burn with fervor; she prayed for ardent and perfect souls in order that they might increase unceasingly in His divine love; she interceded for the souls in Purgatory in order that He might take them quickly to heaven where they can consummate their love that as yet is still fettered in Purgatory; she prayed on behalf of the general and particular needs of Holy Mother the Church that is indeed confided to His care to conserve and increase the spirit of truth and holiness which resides in her alone because of Him; finally, on behalf of all those who live outside the confines of the true Church, and for all the prelates and members of the Church. All this I know with certitude because she submitted everything to my approval."

It seems proper to indicate that the spirituality of this Saint is a magnificent synthesis of contemplative life and apostolic efficacy. Her contemplative life raised her to the dizzy altitudes of Trinitarian life, caused her to feel in her own life the great fertility of the invasion of the Spirit of Love, and it is this invasion of the Holy Spirit, producer of sanctifying grace, which caused her to use her intercessory power, united to Christ, to intercede for the same invasion to occur in the entire Church. The more He Who is the soul of the Church vivified her by inundating her with grace, the holier the Church would become and the more it would reflect the life of Christ. Teresa Margaret devoted herself entirely to begging for the Church the treasures of holiness.

But now we must turn our attention upon the life of love of the Saint. If she had imitated in faith the life of knowledge of the Incarnate Word, rising to the sublimest heights of the contemplative life, she participated no less in His ardent love. Here, above all, her imitation was to cost her a terrific price in fact, a martyrdom caused by the overflow of love that took her, in a remarkably short time, to the most elevated spheres of pure love.

To study this characteristic aspect of the life of the Saint, we have a double source of information. In addition to the depositions of the Process, we have a series of letters that she wrote to her spiritual director during the last months of her life in which she gives him a complete account of the state of her soul. These letters of which we are talking are the eleven letters that were written between the nineteenth of December 1768 and the sixteenth of January 1770, scarcely two months prior to her death. They show us the intimate experiences of the Saint and particularly the pain they caused her. We are inclined to believe, in view of her habitual sobriety, that she was content in these letters to reveal only things that caused her some unrest and that gave rise to various problems for her; everything else she kept to herself. We are treating of a soul that felt itself to be splitting in half: on one side, there was a repugnance that was growing greater instead of diminishing, a repugnance toward every type of good, and on the other side was a need of loving that appeared to be acquiring an ever greater vigor. The testimonies of Father Ildephonse and Mother Anna Maria give us a knowledge of the proportions of this furnace of love that gradually consumed her soul.

But let us first deal with the letters.

In the letter of December 19, 1768, the Saint is under attack: "I am telling you in strict confidence, sure of your discretion, that I find myself in pain because I am not doing anything to correspond to the demands of love. I feel that I am continually being reproached by my Sovereign Good, and yet, I am very sensitive to the slightest movement contrary to the love and knowledge of Him. I do not see; I do not feel; I do not understand anything interiorly or exteriorly that could impel me to love. Everything is an obstacle and prevents me from throwing myself unreservedly into the arms of God, and I am so aware of this fact that I scarcely know how to occupy my mind—

even the very things that could help me to love present obstacles to me, and I strive hard to avoid these. I have no other remedy than to work in complete faith, but on account of my cold-heartedness, this also is painful to me. However, thanks to a continual vigilance over the inferior faculties and over the suggestions of the common enemy (the devil), I think that these things are helping to make me a little less imperfect. For the rest, no one can imagine how terrible it is to live without any love when one is actually burning with the desire for it." This last sentence is a very revealing confession, but the preceding lines indicate that sensitivity [2] was beginning to oppose its inertia to the ardent aspirations of the spirit. We are going to see this scission gradually increase until it actually attains a paroxysm.

The letter of April 1, 1769, shows us that the Saint, after having received detailed direction from her director, put it into immediate practice but without any apparent success: "Your letter was a great consolation to me and gave me much spiritual comfort. The method that you gave regarding the attainment of success in my desires was just what I wanted. I immediately began to obey this advice, and it really seemed to help me a little. Most of the time I had to fight against the current because of the terrific repugnance I felt and also on account of the hardness of my heart. Yet the greatest difficulty does not seem to lie here; it is rather in seeing myself invaded by various fears and surrounded by many temptations, and both to such a point that I sometimes am in doubt as to which way I must turn ... I feel greatly confused; I certainly do not want to offend God. I have no desire other than to belong wholly to Him."

Apparently the devil was trying to upset her but she remained firm in the desire to love.

"This is a torture to me, let alone the fact that it requires such an effort to apply myself to the things of God," she confessed later. "I fear that God is very displeased with my Communions; it seems that I have no desire to ask His help because of the great coldness that I experience.... It is the same with prayer and, of course, in all the other spiritual exercises. I am continually making good resolutions, but I never succeed in attaining some way of successfully overcoming these obstacles that stand in my way and prevent me from throwing myself at His feet." We are inclined to think that the opposition from sensitivity was only increasing, but her efforts became more heroic.

On November 4, 1769, she wrote, evidently under the impression of some great grace: "I try as much as I can not to remain in my failings but to demand instant pardon from God, for I recall that it is time for me to give myself completely to Him.... I ask His pardon for being so distant from Him and I then renew my oblation.... I do all this rapidly and several times a day, but, in spite of it, I often allow myself to be overcome by the extreme coldness I feel. Then comes weakening and lack of confidence—I begin to feel that I shall never attain the heights toward which I tend because the battle within me is so great and I have so little courage in the face of battle.... I try to help myself by making as good a resolution as I can, especially when I feel the greatest repugnance; but in spite of all this, at the first ill wind I find myself thrown on the ground. When I have resolved to conquer my repugnances manfully, the greatest occasions for practicing the newly-made resolutions immediately present themselves— but I lose my courage and the enemy wins the day.... I cannot explain to you the paradoxes that I feel exist within myself. Sometimes I feel the greatest repugnance for performing even the least act of virtue, and I have to do myself the greatest violence in order to perform the act; at other times I want nothing else than to conform myself perfectly with the Heart of Jesus, and then I force myself to practice those virtues that I know will make me especially beloved of that

Heart. At these latter times I try to renew my resolution to suffer and to be silent, but I do not succeed very well, and yet I feel something within me that helps me to remain faithful to God." Here is evidence that the battle was increasing, even to the point that the Saint began to think she was not resisting enough. She remains constant in her resolution to immolate herself in silence. If she finds that she does not succeed, she is under an illusion because we know that those who lived with her thought quite differently.

She insists in her letter of December 6: "My heart is becoming ever more unreceptive of the divine grace that desires to flow into it; I feel myself abandoned and scorned, and I greatly desire the aid of Your Reverence that I will not be lost."

January 16, 1770, the battle is at its peak: "The tempest has become extremely violent, and I feel myself being so knocked about that I scarcely know what to do if this continues. Everywhere there is darkness and danger. My soul is so dark that the very things which used to afford me some spiritual consolation are only a source of torture to me.... I must do violence to myself in order to perform each interior and exterior spiritual exercise.... Finding myself in this state of supreme weariness I commit many failings at each step.... My mind is in such turmoil that it is open to temptations of every sort, especially to those of despair.... I have a great fear of offending God grievously.... I see that I do wrong and at the same time try to follow the inspiration to do good, and then I feel remorse for my infidelity; and to top it all, I am not succeeding in conquering myself because my repugnance is so great."

The sensitivity of the Saint has become so hardened to good that she has the impression of giving in by allowing herself to be delayed by it—hence, the idea that she has fallen into tepidity. But the rest of the letter will show us that she was at the other pole. In spite of the revolt of her sensitivity, her will remained heroically determined to conquer; come what may, she would *be* all God's. "In order to try to conquer myself, I revealed to my superior what causes me to feel so much repugnance, and I have agreed with her to render her an account each day of my infidelities."

She certainly had recourse to great means—little matter that they might be humiliating as long as she arrived at her goal. But to make use of these new means was to cause her additional sorrow. For a long time the superior treated her very harshly. Asked by the Saint herself not to spare her and convinced of her heroic virtue, the superior felt herself urged to act severely and later admitted this to Father Ildephonse. The superior was sick, forced to remain in bed; the Saint took care of her. The sick superior scolded her continually, but the Saint accepted it with the greatest meekness and amiability. The superior was completely ignorant of the interior trials of Teresa Margaret because the Saint had spoken only of her repugnance in the accomplishment of her duties. When she revealed her so-called failings, she had to undergo such harsh treatment that, surprised and hesitant, she asked herself if it were necessary to continue: "For some time I have tried it. When our superior finds me unfaithful she scolds me and threatens punishment if I continue to be so obstinate...." Poor little Saint! She needed no reproaches—she needed encouragement! But God knows what He is doing when He makes His saints. Teresa Margaret confessed that she even interrupted this practice (of rendering an account of her infidelities) and, ever ready to accuse herself, blamed it upon her weakness: "Perhaps the enemy [the devil] sees that I am able to derive a little profit from it. Look; for several days, due to his insinuations, I have omitted making any account." This is only too easy to explain; after all, she needed no new battle grounds upon which to fight. But her heroic virtue embraced everything; Teresa

Margaret had recourse to obedience to conquer: "If you think it good that I continue in doing this, please give me that obedience, and in your charity tell me what things I ought to manifest. Thanks to this obedience I shall be forced to act and I shall no longer give access to my enemy; in this way I shall be acting in the spirit of Our Holy Mother [Teresa of Jesus] who advises us to manifest our interior to our superior regardless of whether or not we reap profit therefrom. In this way also I shall be helped to conquer my repugnances, for until now I have found no means of doing so."

The last section of the letter under discussion shows how Sister Teresa Margaret tried to live up to her ideal ever more perfectly: the ideal of coming to the fullness of love through union with the Heart of Jesus. She asked once again for permission from her confessor to renew her oblation and to "enclose" herself in Him: "I ask for your permission to do it on the morning of the feast of the Purification in imitation of my Mistress, Sister Margaret Mary Alacoque. Our Lord rebuked her for her lack of courage in conquering self for love of Him. She then asked Him what He wished her to do. 'My will (i.e., my inclinations) is stronger than I am,' she said. Jesus answered her: 'Put it into the wound of My Heart, and there it will find the strength necessary to conquer.' Sister Margaret Mary then exclaimed in rapture: 'Ah, my Lord, place it there Yourself, right in the center; so fortify its position there that it will never be able to leave.' If then, Your Reverence is of this opinion, on the morning of the Purification feast I also shall make my offering to the Heart of Jesus through the hands of the Blessed Mother."

We who are already aware of the act of oblation that she had made two years previously can see in this new step of the Saint a heroic application of her will to the goal of belonging completely to God and being consumed by His love. Trial had no effect in her other than to increase her desire to "return love for love."

In the letters that Saint Teresa Margaret wrote to her spiritual director to seek counsel in her trials, we can perceive that the Saint emphasized the trials and shadowed her excesses of love. We can, however, learn about them by reading between the lines. Father Ildephonse will help us in this task by telling us about the sufferings of love and the flames that consumed her heart at the very same time in which she was undergoing this painful martyrdom so well described in her letters. More and more we see that it is a martyrdom caused by an insatiable desire to love.

Constantly, Father Ildephonse calls the torment consuming the Saint a "mortal pain of love" that, in the last two years of her life, made her participate in the same state of soul which caused the Apostle to exclaim: "I desire to be dissolved and to be with Christ!" She experienced, he says, "the terrific agonies of soul that, according to the opinion of Our Holy Mother [Teresa of Jesus], can barely be tolerated unless God comes to the assistance of the soul either by shortening the exile of the soul or by some extraordinary comfort of an external manifestation ... [Note: the Father seems here to be making a reference to the transverberation of the heart of Saint Teresa and the impression of the stigmata upon Saint Francis of Assisi] and our little nun, anxious as she was to keep her secret for God alone, would have never desired a grace like that."

Father Ildephonse continues to give proof of this excess of love that consumed the Saint: he speaks of her extreme horror for sin and any other type of infidelity to God, and it was so great that she would burst into tears at the thought of the ingratitude of sinners. He mentions her astonishing delicacy in the practice of charity, which caused her to renounce the only consolation she had in the midst of her sufferings: consulting her confessor. She deprived herself of this in order to avoid inconvenience to the nun who had to replace her in her duties while she was in the confessional. The good Father again mentions "the terrible agonies that she often spoke of to me, saying that she could no longer live without being able to love God as much as she desired, considering death a great consolation; she therefore asked my permission to ask for it without trying to lessen or escape her sufferings in this life." She was, he says, "almost continually transformed by this love wherein, knowing most clearly the excellence and infinite merit of her Beloved, her love seemed to appear weaker and weaker in her eyes as it actually increased." "The cruelest torturer of her soul," he remarks, "was her love which, in the very same measure that it increased hid itself from the eyes of her spirit. She loved, yet believed she did not; in the measure love grew in her soul, in the same measure augmented the desire of loving and the pain of thinking that she did not love."

Driven on by the desire of giving herself, Teresa Margaret would have liked to have made the most perfect of vows, but, in order to preserve her humility, her confessor pretended that he did not understand what she was talking about. He was also aware that a simple resolution for her assumed the proportions of a solemn vow.

This absolute need of loving finally led her to a paroxysm: to make her consent to her own destruction and to her own eternal unhappiness, as long as she could love.

The testimony of Father Ildephonse is particularly touching on this point: "She made God the most varied offerings in order that He finally make her worthy of loving. Among these different propositions is one that, as I know, became a daily and favorite one: it would not matter to her if she were condemned to hell for all eternity as long as the Lord would grant her the grace to love Him there as much as she wanted to, and then even more than that. I know this with certainty. She repeated this idea several times in my presence, putting all her ardor into it; and oddly, she did it at the same time that she was accusing herself of lukewarmness in love. Prompted by the desire never to allow her to lose any of the beauty of her humility, I told her that everyone ought to be moved by the same sentiments. Shrewdly, I asked her of a sudden: 'Now, supposing that (eternity in hell), what do you think will happen to us if we cannot see God for all eternity and have to suffer from all the horrible torments of the senses?' Resolutely, without any reflection, she answered: 'I think that love would make all things tolerable for us, perhaps even sweet, for love can compass everything.'"

For Saint Teresa Margaret these were not idle words: the will to love God drove her to any conceivable type of folly. We shall soon see this again. For the moment let us content ourselves with the testimony of Mother Anna Maria, who supplements the words of Father Ildephonse with regard to the interior life of the Saint by making mention of her external life during this period.

The Saint never manifested these torments of soul to anyone save her confessors and spiritual directors; during the last year of her life Father Ildephonse was her sole confidant. Mother Anna Maria who, of all the companions of the Saint, knew her best, never knew of these trials, although she did suspect her sufferings: "In the last year of her life one could see on her face that she was undergoing some interior agony, and it was my opinion that it was a question of some spiritual pain. I know for a fact that although she wanted the highest perfection, she never seemed to obtain it in her own eyes. One day I decided to ask her about it. Her answers made me conclude that I had guessed right. Nevertheless, her manner of bearing herself gave me constant cause to admire her. I was aware that everything she did was performed with true fervor of soul; added to this was the fact that during the last year or so that she was with us, her duties became more onerous than those of preceding years, and they included taking care of several sick, fastidious nuns. This was a task to which she added the cheerful accomplishment of many other little things that could help the others. Yet, she never was remiss in her observance and fidelity to community acts.... I am certain that, in the midst of these manifold duties and services, Teresa Margaret acquired an ever-increasing strength and vigor." If love is proved by deeds, we can certainly see it illustrated in our Saint; besides, it is an eloquent testimony to her charity.

Before going any further, let us study the mystical signification of this period of painful trials.

The problem might be stated thus: do we find ourselves confronted with the purifying trial that Saint John of the Cross calls "the dark night of the spirit," or is it merely the question of another type of trial designed to augment her love and its apostolic value? We think that we can with certitude affirm that, in its first stages, the trial of the Saint belonged to the latter period of the night of the spirit but, in its latter stages, it far surpassed it. It would be an error to assert that a revolt or repugnance of sensitivity necessarily denotes a state of soul inferior to the spiritual marriage and contradictory to the demands of the last stages of the night of the spirit.

We know from the works of Saint John of the Cross that there are three steps in this night: the first, darkest of all, is principally characterized by an acute awareness in the soul of her indigence and spiritual misery, while the will at the same time is developing an "estimative" love of God whereby she learns true horror of sin. Then comes a step that is a little less painful wherein the obscure contemplation of God is accompanied by an actual passion of love for Him. Finally, in the third step, the soul enjoys unitive contemplation and fructive love at intervals.

Since 1767 Saint Teresa Margaret had been receiving the first graces of union, and her martyrdom of love was inaugurated at the same time, but it is especially from the last months of 1768 that her trial took the form of an almost insurmountable repugnance of sensitivity that dried up every feeling in the exercise of love and that accentuated her spontaneous impression of being completely devoid of all love.

Saint John of the Cross has clearly indicated that a great prostration of sensitivity accompanies the dark contemplation that purifies the spirit; in the same measure that the spirit becomes lighter, so does the sensible oppression decrease. Yet, with Teresa Margaret, everything is just the opposite: the repugnances and revolt of sensitivity increased during the last weeks of her life in spite of the Trinitarian character of her contemplation that seems to indicate the state of spiritual marriage.

We know that during this period—if we follow teresian and sanjuanistic mysticism [3] unitive mystical contemplation remains uniquely indistinct, "without referring itself to the sacred mysteries"; this is explained by its character of ecstatic paroxysm that does not permit, in the contemplative act, the presence of any given concept which ordinarily seems necessary for contemplation of revealed mysteries. The full maturity and complete balance of the state of the spiritual marriage is not, however, opposed to this type of contemplation.

It is true that the Mystical Doctor (Saint John of the Cross), in two places in his *Spiritual Canticle,* considers it normal that, in this state of spiritual maturity, a complete harmonization of sensitivity with the spiritual part should be had, and this ought to exclude the soul from any suffering arising from disordered impulses of the passions. It follows ultimately that the soul no longer pays attention to the attacks of the devil that are still present in the evil spirit's exaggeration of the movements of this same sensitivity, that is imperfectly dominated and governed by the mind. But if Saint John of the Cross holds that the exclusion of such suffering in the soul that has arrived at the spiritual marriage is normal, he clearly remarks that there are exceptions to the rule. He indicates various reasons for this: at certain times and in certain periods God acts otherwise in the soul and makes it feel things and suffer on account of them, in order that the soul might merit more and grow in fervor, or for other reasons.

In the present case we have plenty of evidence to show that the Saint's experience of the revolt of her sensitivity—and we must not exclude the ordinary diabolic influence exercised in temptation (note that we are in no way thinking of diabolic possession or obsession, but only of the power which the devil can exercise over us in exaggerating the movements of our senses)—provoked a reaction that made her increase immensely in the fervor of "willed" love. The paroxysm present in her soul when she died and in virtue of which she was willing to accept damnation as long as she could love is a convincing proof of it. It would then be abusive and false to interpret this repugnance as a proof of spiritual immaturity.

Saint John of the Cross further teaches, in a very explicit manner, in his commentary on the *Living Flame* that increase of love is possible and normal even in the state of spiritual marriage. The soul, he says, "can qualify herself" and "substantiate herself still more in love." In the commentary on the first strophe he explains how the thrusts of this loving "substantialized" flame cause the soul to aspire for eternal beatitude to the point that she will cry:

"Break the bond of this sweet encounter!"

The soul does this with perfect submission to the divine will; she aspires to a plentitude of perfect love, and this is compatible with her submission. It is necessary that this be so, writes Saint John, for in those moments when the divine flame raises her along with its own movement toward God, "the apparition of glory and love that comes in these touches [and that stop at the portal of the soul without entering since it cannot lodge there due to the narrowness of this earthly dwelling-place] are such that it certainly would be a sign of very little love if the soul did not beg to enter into the perfection and fullness of love."

We know that in these last months Sister Teresa Margaret ardently desired for the "final resolution" that would permit her to love "divinely" as she desired. Father Ildephonse shows us how attached the Saint was to the idea of death as the realization of her only dream. The divine flame she had invoked in her act of oblation consumed her with amazing rapidity and, like a tidal wave, swept her to her goal. The very fact that she did not experience the delightful repast that is the lot of those souls which enjoy the complete harmonization of all their sensitive and spiritual powers actually accentuated her desires and drives. The repugnances and the revolt of sensitivity precisely because they occasioned a stronger reaction to their demands hastened her course toward the "final resolution" with an ever more marked progress. Saint Teresa Margaret is the youngest Saint of the Teresian Carmel;[4] she died at the age of twenty-two years and nine months. If, in spite of her youth, she was able to attain the greatest heights of love, it was because her ascent was of a rapid stride. And, her trial contributed much toward it.

We do not hesitate, therefore, to classify her among the exceptions that the Mystical Doctor explicitly states may occur among souls who arrive at the stage of the spiritual marriage and whose motto might aptly be phrased "to make fervor of love increase."

At the process of beatification Father Ildephonse took the trouble to show that the Saint had come "to that degree of divine union wherein souls can no longer, naturally speaking, continue in this life, but, according to the ordinary ways of divine Providence, receive the invitation to come to enjoy this Sovereign Lord in His unveiled essence and, because of the predilection of His grace, they try with all their power to penetrate the veil even while they remain on this earth in the dark agony of faith."

Father then continues by enumerating his arguments and insists upon the lofty character of the contemplation of the Saint; he recalls her desire to participate in the intellectual operations of the Incarnate Word, a desire which, when realized, led her to "Trinitarian" contemplation. He recalls her high knowledge of the divine attributes, the stability of her union with God in spite of her manifold, distracting occupations; he recalls how she had no longer any need of spiritual books since she was now continually and sufficiently nourished by her own spiritual life. He recalls her delightful purity of conscience and her extreme horror of sin, her complete abandonment and humility in the midst of aridities and interior trials. Finally, he makes mention of the magnanimity that drove her to undertake for God the greatest and most difficult tasks.

This last note, according to the mind of Saint Thomas Aquinas, is the characteristic of the soul that has arrived at that degree of love which he calls *perfectissimus* ("most perfect") to distinguish it from the simple perfect love which marks the entrance of the soul into the unitive way. This *perfectissimus* love is love matured, love proper to the spiritual marriage, love proper to the soul that has attained the last of the "seven degrees of love." We think it useful, at the end of this study, to say something about the heroic magnanimity of this child of twenty-two, who occupied herself with an astonishing exterior activity, completely in the service of her neighbor, during the years she was in Carmel.

She saw in her neighbor a child of God whom she must love for Him and in Him. Her fraternal charity became, in this way, a beautiful confirmation of the reality of her contemplative love. We know for sure that there is only one virtue of charity but that it has a twofold object: God and neighbor. The exercise of either one of these bears eloquent testimony to the perfection of the other. The exercise of fraternal charity is easier to control and thus becomes an excellent criterion of the "truth" in the sentiments of love that animate the soul in its dealings with God.

The fraternal charity that characterized the life of Sister Teresa Margaret in the cloister can be called an "epoch," of which the Lord prepared the ways by His providential dispositions. He intended this to illustrate her heroism in the exercise of Divine Love.

When the Saint entered the cloister, she found herself in a very difficult situation in view of the health of the nuns, from the oldest even to the youngest. We know that two young servant girls were admitted into the monastery (more or less in the capacity of lay-sister postulants) who could be of service there. It is not hard for us to understand the willingness of the superiors to permit those interested in such work to take care of the infirm nuns. From the very dawn of her religious life, and increasing as she remained in the convent, Teresa Margaret profited from the facility in obtaining this permission to practice, almost to an extreme, fraternal charity and devotion.

The needs of the community were even greater when, toward the end of 1767, one of the nuns became a victim of mental disease that eventually became insanity. It was necessary to keep her under lock and key, and care of her consumed several hours.

Beginning in June 1768 Teresa Margaret was given charge of this nun. The Saint already had much responsibility—she was in complete charge of the sacristy due to the illness of Sister Teresa Maria Ricasoli whose assistant she was; she had asked to be permitted to put an octogenarian nun to bed each night, and this deprived her of an hour of her own sleep. She aided Sister Madeleine Teresa Vecchietti, whom she found to be overburdened with tasks, in the surveillance and care of the fruit destined for the meals. She also asked, through the medium of her confessor, to be allowed to care for the insane nun, which certainly consumed a lot of time; she was aware of the demands this would make upon her weak health, but she kept silence about it. One of her most important duties regarding this nun was to bring her her food and to see that she ate it—which consumed more than three hours a day.

This act of charity was accomplished in the midst of invectives and threats. Teresa Margaret controlled her personal terror by having recourse to the Blessed Virgin. Before entering the room of the nun, she would kneel before a statue of the Blessed Mother that was located near the room of the poor Sister and beg courage from the Queen of Heaven. Violent scenes often occurred in which this girl, scarcely twenty years old, showed real heroism. An older nun would watch over her however, to protect her; she would defend the Saint against the too unreasonable exigencies of the demented nun.

The next year saw a change in the scene. This time Teresa Margaret had the job of infirmarian as an office, and the Prioress gave her exclusive care of this unfortunate nun. The superior knew that the Saint would obey her punctually and very exactly, and thus she knew that Teresa Margaret would not give in to all the foolish whims of the nun as long as she had an order to that effect. Mother Prioress therefore gave the Saint such orders and warned her against paying too much attention to the protests of the unfortunate nun.

Unfortunately, the Saint had a companion in the performance of this duty who was older than she and who thought that she ought to have been given precedence in this office. This older nun had much pity for the demented patient and wanted to give in to all her desires. She continually reproached Teresa Margaret for her way of acting, even though the latter was merely obeying the wishes of the superior. Such disagreements are not unusual in religious communities, and they are usually quite painful. The older nun was aware of what would happen should she side with the patient against Teresa Margaret. The patient would become irritated with the Saint; then blows would ensue.

One of the servant-girls mentioned above was a witness of this, but Teresa Margaret made her promise never to speak of it to the Prioress.

Some of the companions of the Saint were aware of the difficult situation; they saw how she was caught between two fires and suggested that she ask the Prioress to permit the older nun to take care of the patient. The Saint replied: "Obedience has confided this work to me, and I cannot reject it." She never brought the matter up to the superior. Her silence was aided by the fact that, at this time, the Prioress herself was confined to bed and thus could not see things for herself.

In spite of the disagreements that occurred each day and in spite of a continual discord which was not her fault, Teresa Margaret surrounded her companion with a light of delicate foresight. She performed the most painful duties toward the demented nun, tried to please her, and then would apologize for not serving her better ... as if she were at fault. Having noticed that the older nun who caused all the trouble liked to stay with the patient, Teresa Margaret, prompted by her compassionate heart, would call the older nun. Sister Madeleine Teresa was aware of the whole situation and saw these delicate tricks of the Saint to give some pleasure to the two of them; she once said to the Saint: "You certainly are very good to be so anxious to see them together when you know that they spend the whole time complaining about you." Teresa Margaret answered: "What do you want? It makes her happy!"—and she added that, since she had not been forbidden to act thus, she could see no reason why she couldn't act this way as long as both parties were happy.

During the last weeks of 1769, the Saint had to devote her entire time to a dying nun. Mother Prioress was forced then to give the older nun complete charge of the insane nun. But as soon as the one nun died, Teresa Margaret resumed charge of the demented patient. We can imagine the irritation of the two friends and the new horrors through which the Saint had to pass.

And never a complaint! The best religious suffered so much in their contacts with the foolish nun that they sometimes felt it necessary to confide their sufferings either to the Prioress or to their confessor. The Saint on the contrary, according to Father Ildephonse, "during the space of nearly two years, which were indeed truly horrible years for her and in which she needed help most, never, as far as I know, mentioned a word about this nun except to excuse her and recommend her to the prayers of the others ... at least, this is the way that she always dealt with me."

While she underwent these painful relations with the foolish nun, the pain of which was heightened by discord with the older companion bound to her by obedience, she also had charge of five seriously ill nuns. Her days were spent in going from one to the other continuously—she scarcely had time to breathe.

It was her desire, in spite of this heavy burden, to be present at all the community acts. She charged the nun whose duty it was to awaken the community in the morning to take extra care in seeing that she was awakened, for she did not trust herself because of her excessive fatigue. Add to this the fact that she was continually practicing corporal mortifications and seeking humiliations and reprimands from her companions.

Who could help but admire the heroism supposed by such a life of continual self-oblation? And still more, in the middle of all this, she had to undergo a tremendous interior martyrdom: the martyrdom of thinking herself a failure in attaining the highest peaks of love. Yet it is this martyrdom that explains everything else and that made everything else possible. To love God, as she conceived of it, Teresa Margaret was quite willing to accept hell for all eternity as long as she could love for all eternity. To Father Ildephonse, who interrupted her on one occasion, she replied that "love itself would make these horrors supportable and even sweet"—the horrors of eternal damnation! These were not vain words: Teresa Margaret knew from experience that love made all things bearable. If, in the middle of a life humanly impossible she remained calm and smiling, it was because an interior flame was consuming her, a flame that obliterated all suffering in its presence, a flame that served as a remedy to her. The Saint was heroic in the gift of herself simply because she was mystically consumed by love.

Her serenity was imperturbable.

"Her face was so peaceful and tranquil that it made everyone think that she had become complete mistress of herself and of all that she did," testifies Sister Teresa Maria Ricasoli, her novitiate companion, and also one of her last patients before her own untimely death. "She appeared to be at the summit of imperturbability" adds Mother Anna Maria. She always acted, according to another witness, "with a truly admirable modesty, never exhibiting the least display of agitation." "We were able to note in her an habitual cheerfulness, a tranquility of spirit and a serenity of countenance that she always showed regardless of how painful the situation in which she found herself might be ... never, so far as I know, had anyone, either myself or another, seen her troubled or moody in any circumstance."

We have a letter of hers dated February 3, 1770, a month previous to her death. She wrote it on the eve of the day on which, no longer able to bear her interior tortures, she sought permission from Father Ildephonse to once again offer herself through the hands of the Blessed Virgin to the Sacred Heart. The letter of which we are speaking shows us that she was preparing a "recreation" for her Sisters. She asked the good priest—who possessed some poetic talent— to compose some couplets for her according to a certain theme: "I have no noteworthy remarks to make on the subject; I wish to tell you, very simply, that the Sisters amuse themselves by joking with me and teasing me, calling me an imp. I wish, as far as I am able, to show them that they are paying me a greater honor to treat me thus, and that, just as they succeeded in making me fall into their trap a few days ago, I too am capable of taking my revenge!" What self-control and self-forgetfulness does such an attitude demand in this child who suffered from an agony of love that would soon bring her to her grave and who forgot herself in order to try to amuse her companions with a recreation.

Her death indeed was near. We are inclined to think that she had a presentiment of it.

Several days before her death Teresa Margaret wrote her father a letter in which she enclosed a picture of the Sacred Heart, which she herself had mounted upon a white background. It was to be a last reminder, a souvenir, of their daily rendezvous in the Heart of Jesus. She also begged her father to make a novena for her. She gave no reason for this, but there is every indication that she had her death in mind.

During these last few days she confessed herself unworthy of being in Carmel.

On March 4 she made her last confession. She intended that it be a "special" confession and Father Ildephonse went along with the idea. The compunction of the Saint was very great; she wept but upon leaving the confessional she had regained her usual composure.

That evening on her knees she begged an old religious to correct her faults.

The next day she received Holy Communion as Viaticum and it was her last Communion.

The sixth passed as usual. In the evening, toward the end of meditation, Teresa Margaret began to make her rounds of the sick. It was near six o'clock. She spent a little time with Mother Prioress who had chronic leg trouble. Then she went to see Sister Teresa Maria Ricasoli, a permanent invalid, and consoled her by quoting some nice thoughts from a book by Father Binet, S.J. These quotations were concerned with conformity to the Divine Will. She performed several small services for the cripple and then went to the refectory.

By this time the community had already finished its supper and had departed. Teresa Margaret sat down to eat her meager repast. It was Lent, and since the Lenten collation is made up of bread and dried fruit, it took little time to eat it.

Suddenly Teresa Margaret was shaken by a violent pain in the abdomen. She arose and left the refectory, but she was forced to stop at the first cell. There she knelt for a short time at the side of the bed and then tried to get to her own cell that was on the same floor. She was unable to do this and was forced to call another nun, who happened to be passing at the moment, to come to her aid. This religious ran to her, found her lying on the floor, and helped her to get on the bed. By this time several of the other nuns had come upon the scene, and Teresa Margaret begged her surprised companions to recite the "Glory be" five times in honor of the Sacred Heart. The doctor, who had been summoned immediately, did not think that her situation was a grave one and contented himself with prescribing a few remedies.

During the night one of the servant-girls stayed with the Saint, who was very anxious not to have the other religious staying with her since she wanted them to get their rest. She told this servant-girl to be very careful to make no noise, so as not to disturb the nuns. Teresa Margaret spent the night in terrible pain. She was constantly reciting the psalm "Miserere."

The next day the doctor ordered a bleeding. The surgeon who performed this operation sensed the gravity of the situation and was of the opinion that special care was needed. But since the doctor of the community had seen nothing alarming in the condition of the young nun, the religious to whom he confided his opinion said nothing for fear of alarming the community. She contented herself with asking Mother Prioress to beg the other religious in the city to pray for Teresa Margaret.

The suffering seemed to be easing up a little, but the truth was, gangrene was setting in.

Teresa Margaret held her crucifix in her hands and kissed it frequently. She asked another Sister to put an image of the Sacred Heart on the wall near the bed. She was very pleased when this had been done, but, fearing that it might be soiled, she asked that the picture be returned to its former position.

The Saint was rapidly approaching her last moment on earth, but no one was aware of it.

The same situation existed with regard to what was occurring in her soul; no one realized the violent love which was consuming her and which caused her to cry to heaven: "Break the bonds of this sweet encounter!"

From earth Teresa Margaret received nothing but silence, complete solitude.

Mother Anna Maria was present but divined nothing of the mystery of love working in the soul of the dying nun. Only Father

Ildephonse knew, and he was not there. He was not to be present to receive the last confidences of the Saint. Our Lord wanted to make her an example of the hidden life, a model for souls who immolate themselves for His eyes alone; so, He kept for Himself the solemn moment of her departure for heaven.

About three o'clock in the afternoon a sudden spasm marked a renewed outbreak of illness. Someone hurried to the Church where the extraordinary confessor of the convent was hearing the confessions of the nuns. He brought the Holy Oils ... but it was too late. A conditional absolution, extreme unction "in extremis" and ... all was finished.

The grief of the nuns was intense. Everyone was shaken by this unexpected catastrophe. Yet, when they were going to bury the body, an unexpected thing occurred. Immediately after death it had become greatly swollen, but at this moment it returned to normal and became exceedingly beautiful. The Episcopal Curia ordered that the body not be buried immediately. The earthly glorification of the Saint had begun.

Several days later Father Ildephonse was walking with Father John of the Cross who had been the ordinary confessor of the Saint from September 1767 until May 1769. The two religious were discussing her untimely death.

"In our conversation about the Servant of God who had died a few days previous," Father Ildephonse recalls, "I expressed my opinion in terms that I still remember very well: 'I think that Sister Teresa Margaret, even if she had no corporal malady, could not have lived very much longer, so great was the strength of the love of God in her.' Then the good Father, turning his eyes upward as one does when his opinion is voiced by another just as he is about to give it, answered me with feeling in his voice: 'Blessed be God, I also am thinking the same.'"

These two Fathers who had known her best during the last years of her life were of the opinion that the Saint had died of love. "I have always thought," adds Father Ildephonse, "and I still do, that the premature death of the Servant of God was caused more by the secret violence of love than by her short illness, or perhaps, the illness was caused by the force of her love."

Thus we see the teachings of Saint John of the Cross on the death of love being attributed to the Saint. He attributes this special kind of death to persons who have arrived at this life of transforming union: "If other persons die of sickness or fullness of age, these, more than dying from that type of death, add to it an impulse and overflowing of love, the like of which they have never received previously, and this breaks the bond and crowns the soul." Natural causes for the death are not scorned by the Mystical Doctor, but he does not consider them to be the final determinant of the death: the cause of death is the flood of the soul's love rushing toward God.

Certainly, sickness did its work in Teresa Margaret; but more powerful was her immense desire for the fullness of love, which was fired in her by the Holy Spirit, and it was this that precipitated her into eternity. We have every reason then to affirm that Saint Teresa Margaret died a death of love.

Saint Teresa Margaret was the victim of divine "consuming love." She had expressed in the practical formula, "to render love for love," the lesson of love that she had learned in her youth, thanks to diligent meditation upon the revealed truths of the Faith. One day God Himself gave her the full meaning of this formula when He caused her to feel what it is to love divinely and to be loved divinely.

New horizons had been opened before her wonder-struck eyes on that occasion. She felt herself being drawn toward them, but the closer she seemed to get, the further away they seemed to be. This "frustration" gave rise to an inexpressible agony of suffering within her: that of not loving as she wished and knew she must.

By instinct she knew that only the transformation of love caused by the overflowing of the Holy Spirit into her soul could realize her goal; she therefore offered herself as a victim to be consumed by Him, begging Jesus, her Priest, to obtain the divine flame of love for her.

And, what is more, the flame actually did increase in her, gradually taking possession of her and causing within her an intense torment of insatiable love.

Stirred by inertia and the revolt of sensitivity that bore heavily upon her soul, this insatiable love lost all patience and revealed exigencies which only fostered greater abandonment to the divine wishes: provided that she could love as she felt she must, Teresa Margaret would accept anything...even hell!

The flame that consumed the Saint was implacable. Teresa Margaret was never to know the respite of having the interior harmony that is common to transformed souls. The revolt of her sensitivity would make more vertiginous her course toward the final flowering of love, realized only in heaven.

In the center of this life of love, we find the mystery of Jesus and His Divine Heart. It was in contemplating the Sacred Heart that Saint Teresa Margaret learned the great lesson that was to guide her during her entire life: to return love for love. It was in considering the Sacred Heart that she learned how to do this. The Sacred Heart was always her model.

When the horizons of mystic love with all its possibilities of love were opened before her eyes, it was still in the Heart of Jesus that she sought the means: desiring to "live with Him, in Him, and by Him" the same life of love that was His. She understood that this Divine Heart is inhabited by the Holy Spirit, that it is His "chosen tabernacle," and she begged Jesus to give her the Spirit of Love by consuming her with this divine flame.

Completely absorbed in Jesus and the beauties of His soul, Teresa Margaret desired only one thing: to participate in His love: to participate in His knowledge that plunged His intellect into the mystery of the Trinity. She felt it her vocation to "emulate in faith (as far as it was permitted a creature) the sublime knowledge and affections of the most holy Humanity of Jesus Christ, united hypostatically to the Word." Indeed, Teresa Margaret became a profoundly Trinitarian soul, and at the heights, which she had desired so long, we see united in her the mystical—yet revealing—contemplation of the mystery that is the center of all spiritual life. It was toward the Trinity, One yet Triune, that, under the inspiration of the Holy Spirit, the insatiable love of the Saint arose with a ceaseless drive that consumed her in a short time and that finally threw her into the furnace of divine love.

She went *from the Sacred Heart to the Trinity,* and the hidden life taught her the way.

In love with the hidden life, Teresa Margaret saw Jesus as her model. Her penetration into the intimate sanctuary of the soul of Christ revealed to her the way that led to the Father and to the Trinity and actually transformed the disciple of Margaret Mary into a Mistress of the spiritual life. She teaches us how, after rising to the heights of the Trinity, we can come down to the aid of the Church and of souls by devotion to the Holy Spirit. Teresa Margaret has realized, in a most practical way, the most elevated and most efficacious synthesis between the contemplative life and the active life. From this fact we are permitted to consider her as a person of the first rank in the file of the great "supernatural" saints.

The spiritual itinerary of Saint Teresa Margaret was both sublime and limpid. A word suffices to characterize the work of love in this great soul—we are forced to agree with Father Ildephonse who really knew her better than anyone else—"The Lord Thy God is a consuming fire." (Dt 4:24)

Notes

[1] Hebdomadary" is the one assigned to intone various sections of the Office for the space of a week.

[2] In the *Dark Night,* book 2 chapter 8 Saint John of the Cross indicates the meaning of the term "sensitivity" used by Father Gabriel in this article. The Mystical Doctor speaks of the night of the spirit darkening "the soul according to its faculties and desires, both natural and spiritual." This means, in the case of Saint Teresa Margaret, that all which was natural in her rebelled against the onslaught of the supernatural which God was infusing into her soul.

[3] We can remark that in Saint John of the Cross, mystical contemplations of the Incarnate Word and mystical participation in the Trinitarian life are reserved for souls who have come to the spiritual marriage. Likewise in Saint Teresa, contemplation of the Trinitarian mystery belongs to the seventh mansion of the "Interior Castle."

[4] Editor's Note: This affirmation, while true at the time this study first appeared, is now superseded by Pope John Paul II's canonization of Saint Teresa of the Andes in 1993. She died north of Santiago, Chile in 1920 at the age of 19 years and 9 months.

The Institute of Carmelite Studies promotes research and publication in the field of Carmelite Spirituality. Its members are Discalced Carmelites, part of a Roman Catholic community—friars, nuns, and laity—who are heirs to the teaching and way of life of Teresa of Jesus and John of the Cross, men and women dedicated to contemplation and to ministry in the Church and the world. Information concerning their way of life is available through local diocesan Vocation Offices or from the Vocation Directors' Offices:

1233 So. 45th Street, W. Milwaukee, WI 53214

P.O. Box 3420, San Jose, CA 95156-3420

5151 Marylake Drive, Little Rock, AR 72206